Journey of
Healing

Leaving the
Broken Road

Journey of Healing Series: Book Three

Robert G. Longpré

Retired Eagle Books

March, 2019

Dedication

Though we may think that we do the work of healing on our own, the truth is that there are always others who make the journey with us. My wife, Maureen and my three children, Noelle, Natasha, and Dustin, have all had a vital part in the process of helping me put the broken pieces of my psyche back together. This book is dedicated to them. This book is also dedicated to my seven grandchildren: Devon, Hunter, Cameron, Griffin, Talan, Grayson, and Sophie, in hopes that they learn that it is okay to be broken. The pieces can be welded back together making them stronger with the help of family, friends, and mental-health professionals. This book is also for everyone who needs to put the pieces back together again, and for those who support them from the sidelines.

Robert G. Longpré

"whatever reality may be, it will to some extent be shaped by the lens through which we see it". – James Hollis, Jungian Analyst, The Middle Passage, 1993.

Retired Eagle Books
Box 423 Elrose,
Saskatchewan, Canada S0L 0Z0

ISBN-13: 978-1-989019-08-5

3

Table of Contents

4

Introduction

The sky is wild this morning. One moment it is dark with ominous clouds flying by as if they are on a freeway, and the next moment there is glorious sunshine without a cloud to be seen. The speed at which this is all happening makes the mind swirl. Sometimes nature serves as a good metaphor for what is happening within one's psyche. I know that in today's case, nature mirrors the stormy seas within me.

I didn't sleep well, and it wasn't because of the rain overnight, or the wind. Rather, it was because of the stirring of the darkness that is still within me, the stuff that lies below the surface of conscious awareness, in a place called the unconscious. In this unconscious world, which I usually access at night in dreams, I usually find myself as both the hero and the villain. And when I wake up, I wonder about those dreams that leave me more exhausted than rested.

Because of my involvement with depth psychology, I knew that answers did exist, somewhere deep within me, my answers. This morning, as I sat on our upper balcony in Ecuador, our annual escape from winter in Canada, my wife and I once again talked about this book which has been the source of my agitation for the past several days. That disquietude within me had been stealing my sleep. As we talked, it became evident that I needed to start this book again from the beginning. I needed to tell it from the first-person voice, my voice. As well, I needed to step outside the story from time to time to explain to the reader what was working beneath the surface of my own awareness. I allow my counsellor voice to explain what was stirring below. In a way, it is returning to the structure of the first book in this series.

As a child I was sexually abused, emotionally abused, and physically abused by both parents and others. The sexual abuse extended to include my maternal grandfather and more than one parish priest. I was a docile child, the eldest of nine children. I had written the story of that childhood and so realised that it not necessary to repeat that story all over again. As I understood it, while growing up it was my job to please others, to take care of others, to put others before myself. I forgave my parents for their part in the abuses before they both passed away, unspoken forgiveness for we never really talked about what had happened.

The behaviour patterns I learned in early childhood, continued until years after I was married with children of my own. I carried over the patterns, which influenced how I interacted within the family in which I was husband and father. The patterns carried over into a career as an educator, coach and then as counsellor to students, staff and people from within the community. I was well trained to put others first and do my utmost best to be a good father, a good husband, brother-in-law, coach, counsellor and neighbour. This was a story, a role, and an identity I knew well, one that I wrestled with through midlife and psychoanalysis and therapy.

Now, in my sixties, I am returning to finish the story begun in the first two books of this series, and reclaim my identity, and psyche as best I can. I am a man, not a child-victim of sexual abuse continuing to seek approval, seeking to please others while disregarding my "*self.*" Again, I will use fictitious names for all involved though the story really did happen as it is told in these pages. All that is, except for my name.

This book charts the journey of healing that I followed, a path that has allowed me to finally reach a place of calm and peace. Each person who makes their own journey of healing must listen to their inner voice, as well as their body to find the right way forward. The goal is healing, not meeting the needs and expectations of others. My journey cannot be your journey of healing. However, you might find something of value in my story. If something resonates, listen to that and explore it. If it grates against everything, also listen to that. Above all, dare to do what is needed to heal yourself.

Robert G. Longpré, February 2019

Part One

Ignorance is Bliss

"We are all socialized to serve and maintain the collective, family structures and social institutions that have a life of their own but require the repeated sacrifice of the individual to sustain them."

James Hollis – Under Saturn's Shadow

The story of love and marriage begins, and the past disappears. Trauma buried in the shadows, slips from consciousness allowing one to invest fully in relationship, career, and life. The small cracks allow only tiny disruptions in an otherwise happy life.

Chapter One – A Married Man in Edmonton

Our marriage photo from August 28, 1971

With the arrival of spring and the disappearance of the snow in 1971, Marynia and I would wander alone through the pastures and woodlands of her parents' pioneer farmstead. I took this rare time while we were alone, to shed my clothing to enjoy the sunshine. Marynia thought it was a bit strange, but simply accepted my nudity without question. She walked hand in hand with me through the fields as if we were Adam and Eve in the Garden of Eden. After all, she was in love with me.

We had lived together from the time I had moved into the farm home in early December 1970. The house was shared with a few of her older brothers. There was always someone in the house. The lack of privacy was something I was used to, as I had never had any privacy while growing up as the eldest of nine children. Though I would have preferred that we had more private time and space, the reality dictated that we lived communally with these brothers and their friends.

That first winter with Marynia introduced me to Ukrainian culture. Both of her parents had been born in the Ukraine and had emigrated to Canada. The house was old, pioneer old. Yet within it, the latest of sound equipment blasted out sounds of rock music and protest songs. In between sublime sessions of listening to music, and then performing our own versions of these latest sound tracks and doing chores, I was learning to take my place among Marynia's family. Two of Marynia's brothers were musicians. Maksym played bass guitar, Eugene played lead guitar, a friend named Horace played drums, and I played rhythm guitar and sang most of the vocals.

That first spring together as lovers and life-mates had been celebrated as it was celebrated by other young lovers throughout human history. We simply trusted and followed the lead of the other. We explored the countryside together. I learned about her family history, the land, and the daily rhythms of farm life. Marynia learned about my willingness to try all that was asked of me.

The uncomplicated life on the farm allowed me to return to writing. I published four editorials in the local newspaper and began experimenting with fiction. I hadn't written anything the previous few years following high school. Seeing my words in print, with my name attached was an accomplishment that had me wanting more.

Late in the spring, at Marynia's prodding, I agreed to have her meet my parents and siblings. As spring turned into early summer, I phoned home and told my mother we would be in

Ottawa, giving her the date of our arrival by train. Though I hesitated in giving advance notice of our arrival, I needed someone to meet us at the train station and give us a ride to our family home, which was on acreage near Bell's Corner. When we got off the train, it was my father who met us.

"So, this is the young woman you left home for," remarked Laurent. "I'm Laurent," he said while offering his hand to Marynia. "No wonder Bobby fell in love with you."

I hated being called Bobby, and he knew it. I had always wanted to be called Robert while I was growing up. With most people outside of the family I was Robert. Within the extended family, I had comfortably settled for being called, Bob. Being called Bobby left me feeling as though I was still considered a child.

We arrived in the yard. It looked like no one was taking care of the yard and that no one cared anymore. When I had left home, the yard had been in good order. Now, it had gone wild. My mother, Betsy, met us at the door with a smile. As soon as I introduced her to Marynia, she turned to Laurent and gave him a beaming smile dismissing both Marynia and me. Her husband was home. My brothers and sisters were all present, except for Keith who wasn't living at home anymore. I introduced them to Marynia. I was pleased how they all were so welcoming of her, a sharp contrast from my mother's welcome. With my mother focused on my father, I felt I had turned invisible for both of them. In a way, that felt good. In the past I had dreaded being noticed by my parents, as it typically resulted in pain.

When the initial excitement had settled down, Marynia and I were given my old bedroom to use. The room was now Béatrice's room. I knew it had been her idea, rather than my mother's. Though my mother didn't work, she had never invested much time or energy in the house. Things either never got done, or were done by her children.

The first thing I did when we took our bags into the small bedroom, was to check out my book collection which had been left behind. I was surprised to see that most of the books were gone. Béatrice had exchanged most of them for romance novels, which lay scattered all over the room. Béatrice had never been one to keep a tidy and organised room. As I searched, I found a few of my books were still there, my most important books: The Prophet, Thus Spoke Zarathustra, The Divine Comedy, and a few novels by Tolstoy and Dostoyevsky. My record collection was gone. I sighed and accepted the losses as I had when I had lived at home.

Once we had put our bags in the bedroom, we had a few moments to ourselves. I looked at Marynia with a question mark in my eyes. She answered quietly, "I didn't know that your family was so poor." For a moment, I felt ashamed that she had to see the truth. See saw my response and quickly gave me a hug. Despite my roots, she still wanted me, still loved me.

Then, my mother called out: "Bobby, can you make Dad and I some tea." It wasn't a question, but a command.

Out of habit, I replied without thinking, "Yes, Mom."

"Make sure to use the good china and bring it up when it's ready."

"Yes, Mom."

Marynia went with me into the kitchen and was appalled by what she saw. Dirty dishes were everywhere. Knowing Béatrice, I looked and found more dishes stuffed into the stove oven. Though Marynia's pioneer home was made of logs, mud and straw, the place was always clean, even when it was just her and her brothers living in it. Once the kettle of water had been put on the stove, Marynia helped me clean up the kitchen. While we worked together, the children had returned to watching television, except the older boys who had gone out to hang out with their friends.

With tea finally made, I put the teapot, cups and saucers, sugar cubes, and carnation milk onto a tray. I had had a lot of practice in being my mother's servant. I carried the tray upstairs, while Marynia finished the last of the cleaning in the kitchen. As soon as I got to the top of the stairs, I was glad that Marynia hadn't come up with me. My parent's bedroom door was left open and I could see my father giving my mother oral sex. My mother grinned at me, pleased to have a witness that her husband still loved her. Without saying a word, I set the tray down in the hallway before returning downstairs.

"What's the matter, Bob?" Marynia asked when she noticed the pallor on my face.

"Nothing," was all I could muster in response. Wanting to deflect her concern, I remarked, "I think we deserve that cup of tea now that the kitchen is cleaned. Let's take it into the dining room."

Marynia knew that something was bothering me, and she was disappointed that I didn't want to talk about it with her. She hated secrets. It was as if I didn't trust her with my feelings.

The rest of the day passed in a blur as I became more and more silent. Marynia had discovered a pail of unwashed diapers in the washroom and shook her head feeling sorry for me. She now understood why I never talked about my past. At some point Marynia knew she was going to get me to talk about my past. However, for now, she decided to simply be there for me. After all, it was only a visit. She planned that when we got back to the farm in Saskatchewan, she would encourage me to tell my stories of growing up.

Besides having Marynia meet my parents and see firsthand, the conditions in which my siblings still lived, conditions that existed when I was a child at home, I introduced her to some of my other family members, including my English grandfather, my French grandparents, and an assortment of aunts, uncles, and cousins. The visit wasn't intended to be a long visit. The whirlwind of visits allowed her to see a broader picture of my extended family. It wasn't long before we left to return to the Canadian prairies and the farm in Saskatchewan.

With the decision to follow through with that initial promise of marriage in September of 1970, I knew I needed to get a job. Marynia had told me when I proposed that she wouldn't get married until after her twenty-first birthday. That left me six weeks to find a job, and a home for us to live in, wherever the job would be found. The last thing I wanted to do was to follow in the footsteps of my father, who had issues with keeping a job. Welfare had been a common solution that my parents had used to navigate the poverty that came from those periods of unemployment.

Seeing an advertisement in a newspaper for provincial civil servant jobs in Edmonton, Alberta, I felt confident that this was going to be my chance to get a steady job, a respectable job. My confidence was based on my having worked for the Federal civil service in Ottawa. It had been more than a year since I had a haircut. Because I was unwilling to cut it, we travelled to Regina to buy a short-haired wig. My long hair had become a part of my identity. Modelling the wig, I saw a different man staring back at me from the mirror. This was a man that a government personnel manager would likely hire. Without the wig, I looked like a long-haired dreamer, not a dependable employee.

I travelled alone to Edmonton on a Greyhound bus. I wrote the civil service exam and was immediately hired following an interview with the personnel manager. I had worn the wig through all parts of the process, projecting the image of myself as a clean cut, conservative young man. I had successfully become a clerk in the Department of Social Services for Alberta. I returned to the farm to gather my few belongings, mostly books and a few records. Marynia packed her bag with clothing. Then, the two of us returned to Edmonton. Marynia suggested that we could stay with her eldest sister, Margaret, until we found our own place.

I had a new job as a civil servant in Edmonton, and Marynia soon found a job working at a corner grocery store as a clerk. The money we earned had gone into paying rent for our basement apartment on Whyte Avenue, and for a few pieces of furniture: two chairs, a tiny kitchen table for two, a basket chair for the living room, as well as a few cement blocks and wooden planks to serve as shelving in the living room. The bedroom a mattress on the floor was all the furniture we needed. It was the beginning of making the place our own home. We were young and in love, and we didn't need any more than these few things and each other. It was the first time we had lived together without someone else sharing the living space with us. The world looked and felt perfect. We were soulmates, perfect partners.

Four weeks later, on August 28, 1971, we got married. Wearing a purple shirt with a tie and blue jeans, with my long hair falling in waves, I looked at the long, golden-haired goddess dressed in white who had just repeated, "I do," to the Justice of the Peace. We were now man and wife. Marynia loved me. We were married two days after Marynia's twenty-first birthday.

"Thanks, Mom and Dad," Marynia spoke, with her voice filled with emotion following a gift of two hundred dollars. "You didn't need to give us anything," she protested. "Just having you here is the best wedding gift of all."

Two weeks later, I rode my bicycle over a cliff while showing off to my new bride. I had accordioned my bicycle and compressed my back. I had shrunk an inch, narrowly escaping death by mere inches. I soon recovered and two weeks later, I returned to work. The accident soon faded into the background as one of the dumb things a person does in life.

With encouragement from me, Marynia applied for a civil service job with the Forestry Service when the grocery store job came to an end. With her new job as a civil servant, we were finally able to begin saving some money. My accident had persuaded both of us to be better prepared for tough times in the future. One never knew who would be out of work for any number of reasons. Fear of poverty drove both of us to work hard regardless of whether we liked the job.

Marynia's brother, Maksym, who was often mistaken as my brother because of our similar size, complexion, and personality, came to live with us for the autumn. His job had relocated to Edmonton. With Maksym sharing the rent, life became economically easier for us. It did mean a loss of freedom in being alone, but the benefits seemed to be worth it, especially for Marynia. It helped fill in the silent spaces I created.

In the spring of 1972, we moved across the river to live closer to our work. One of the side effects of the move into a modern apartment tower, was a shift within me. Strangely, I became even quieter. I began to go out jogging. At first, Marynia and Maksym would go running with me. We always did everything together. However, it wasn't long before I began to find myself running alone, running faster and longer.

Something was brewing beneath the surface. Something that appeared to have been triggered by my brother, Keith's visit to our home. Keith came wearing his military uniform, telling us about his medical discharge. It wasn't long before Keith wanted money to help him through some tough times. Despite his apparent need, Keith considered himself a better man than me. As he reminded me, more than once during his visit, he had served his country while I had been living like a hippy. Keith had adopted our father's attitude of entitlement. I refused giving him help. I knew that I would only find myself falling back into the old patterns of feeding the needs of others at my own expense. I had a wife now and she didn't deserve this version of me as her husband. And then he left. With his departure, I found myself compelled to run.

Aside from momentary glitches in my personality and behaviour, life was near perfect. Marriage suited both of us. Love bridged the glitches.

Chapter Two – Reaching For Dreams

Growing vegetables on the family farm, summer of 1973.

Our first year of marriage was a journey of shared dreams and successes. Though we both worked for the provincial government, neither of us felt that our jobs amounted to anything more than making a living. We didn't hate our jobs, but somehow, we both felt that there had to be something more. It was in the telling each other of our hopes and dreams, when we began to plan for making our lives and jobs more meaningful. I had spoken to Marynia about my desire to become a teacher, a dream from when I was a high school student. Her dreams were of a family and of a career in some area of medicine. Looking realistically at these dreams,

Marynia wisely suggested that we begin with my becoming a teacher. Our future dreams would follow from that first step.

Because we had lived frugally, with Maksym sharing the living costs, and because both of us had civil servant jobs, we had been able to save quite a bit of money. Though we could have spent it on furniture and entertainments, we chose to put our money away in savings. With the first days of spring sunshine, we saw that we had more money in the bank than either had ever had in the past. Marynia encouraged me to follow my dream of becoming a teacher. I saw the hope, pride, and belief in me, in her eyes, a belief that I didn't want to ever betray. And so, with her encouragement, I sent out letters to a few universities, including the University of Notre Dame.

In late May, Marynia raced to give me a letter which had just arrived. "Bob, it's from Notre Dame University!" she exclaimed, filled with hope. Opening the letter, with Marynia watching intently, the door to my future as a teacher had opened.

"They've accepted me," I crowed with a relief. "I only have to take an extra Math course as a mature student."

I didn't waste any time in applying for a student loan from the Federal Government. Together with Marynia, we began to prepare for the move to Nelson, British Columbia. We had decided to stay in an apartment, in residence. Knowing that Maksym would likely return to live with us for the winter, we signed up for a two-bedroom apartment on campus.

"We'll need to get a vehicle," Marynia announced in early July 1972. "Ivan told me that he found a good half-ton that would be perfect for us, a Ford. What do you think, Bob? He said we could get it for only fifteen hundred dollars. We could move our stuff to Nelson in the truck, as well as having a way to get to Wynyard to see my parents during school breaks."

Ivan was Marynia's oldest brother, a man who was the same age as my father, and who like my father had served in the Korean War. Ivan was an auto insurance adjuster who had connections with an auto-body repair shop in Fort St. John, British Columbia.

Smiling at Marynia's excitement, I replied without hesitation, "That's awesome! You're sure that we can afford it, with me going to school and all? You do realise that I don't have a driver's licence, right?"

"We can afford it, especially since you'll be getting the student loan. Don't worry, I'll get you ready for your driver's licence when we're back in Wynyard."

One year after beginning my job with the Department of Social Services in Edmonton, I handed in my resignation. We drove to Nelson, picked out our apartment, met a young couple across the hall from our place, and a second, older couple, also in the same residence block. We wasted little time making the place our home.

A few days before the classes at the university were to begin, Marynia and I were taking our first walk through the small city of Nelson. She was wearing a long dress that evoked the image of a European Lady from the distant past. Her long, straight hair framed her oval face, which had been graced with a perpetual smile. I took a photo of her smiling on the bridge as she waved at me, one of many that captured her smile. No sooner had I taken the photo, when Marynia cried out:

"My ring! Oh, my ring!" she screamed as she pointed to the water flowing under the bridge. As though paralyzed with the loss of her ring, she froze at the railing looking into the water as her tears flowed. "Bob, you've just got to find it."

I had already run down the bank to the creek and waded into the water. The creek was less than a foot deep. I searched for a glint of gold, hoping that the bright sunlight would help me locate the ring. I had guessed well at where the ring should have landed. The ring's weight had kept it from being swept away by the flowing creek waters. There it was, nestled beside a rock, waiting to be retrieved.

Quickly rescuing the ring, I called out, "It's okay, Marynia. I have it. I have your ring." Rushing back to her, I placed the ring on her finger as I had a year earlier. The ring she had never taken off since our marriage.

With no expectations of what life was supposed to be like in the university town, the two of us explored the community and the surrounding trails along the slopes of the mountain, and along paths bordering the creeks. It was a golden time filled with sunshine and high hopes for our future. A few days after the start of classes, Marynia got a job at a local bank. Life was getting better and better.

Living alone once again, I felt a strange sense of freedom. I dared to risk being myself. I got permission to paint our apartment. The university paid for the paint which I picked out, and I created a panorama of shapes in contrasting colours on the walls of our apartment. As I painted while Marynia was at work, I was nude. I used the excuse to myself that I was simply protecting my clothing. In reality, it was as if I was back in Vancouver with Sandy where we both painted scenes on the walls of our attic room. We never wore clothing in that attic room within which we lived for just over a month. It was an unconscious return to a rare time of private freedom.

Three weeks into the first term, with assignments completed, Marynia and I headed out into the low mountains near Nelson, to wander down new trails, and enjoy the tranquillity of the forest. Without thinking about it, I slipped out of my clothing when we stopped to rest on a rock bathed in sunshine. It was a private moment far away from anyone who might see us. We simply sat side-by-side and it was enough. We were in love. Marynia accepted the moment, as she had before when we were walking the pastures near the home farm. She didn't understand why I was nude. It was enough that I had kept it private, with her as the only witness.

Six weeks into the term, I was excused from continuing to take the non-credit Math class. I had achieved a mark in the nineties, and an equally as high mark in the credit-level Math class I was taking at the same time. I was no longer classified as a mature student. I had earned the right to be a full-fledged student based on merit alone.

"Wow!" Marynia exclaimed, when I told her the news that afternoon when she returned from the bank. "That's incredible news, Bob."

"Thanks, Marynia. I knew that I was able to do it, but it feels good to be able to prove it."

A few days later, a fire alarm woke us in the middle of the night. Without thinking about it, we both reacted immediately by leaving the building. I had grabbed a shirt which was by the door as I exited. Moments later, we were standing outside the building with a few other couples. Marynia and I were the only ones without clothing. I gave Marynia my shirt which helped provide her with some cover from the eyes of others. Most of the students in the building were poking their heads out windows, pointing at those of us who stood outside and laughing. It was a false alarm, something that was not too uncommon at that time of year. The only people outside with us were other first year students. It was an embarrassing moment that was the only glitch in an otherwise perfect autumn in Nelson.

The first real snowfall of the year came several weeks after the fire-alarm incident. Marynia and I were invited to go to a party at my Sociology professor's home. His home was on the side of the mountain to the north of Nelson. Most of those attending the party weren't students. Only three married student-couples were invited. We caught a ride with one of the other married couples, Tom and Theresa, and a university staff member who lived near the campus. Tom and Theresa had become our best friends in Nelson. Like Marynia and I, they were mature young adults, rather than fresh out of high school.

The professor's house on the side of the mountain was large, a log house with a fireplace and a huge living and dining area that was filled with people. The hostess took Marynia's potluck contribution, and that of Theresa, and placed them on the table with the other meal dishes. Marynia had made a casserole dish filled with perogies, with a bowl of creamed mushroom sauce to be used with the perogies. There was no way a person would be able to sample everything that had been placed on the table.

As the evening wore on, and people were beginning to leave, our host announced that it was time for the Finnish Sauna. He invited those who wanted to experience a Finnish Sauna to join him and his wife in the sauna. The sauna was in a separate building about fifteen metres from the house. The sauna rules required that all participants be nude when in the building. This apparently, was the norm for Finnish saunas all over the world.

Curious, and with Marynia's agreement, we joined those taking part. It was full night outside, pitch-black dark. With only the dim light within the sauna itself, and the light coming from the cabin's windows, it was easy to take part in the event. The darkness concealed more than it exposed. As well, with everyone else in the same state of undress, Marynia became less nervous. The heat was luxurious. Soon sweat was cascading down our bodies, a contrast to the winter chill we had experienced while walking from the house to the sauna while nude.

When it was obvious that most had had enough heat, the host suggested a quick roll in the snow with the option of making snow angels, before heading back to the house to claim clothing and calling it a night. The sauna was the host's version of a winter's night cap.

Laughter filled the mountainside. Marynia soon convinced me to return to the sauna so that she could warm up before we got dressed and returned home. I had revelled in the freedom of the Finnish Sauna shared with Marynia and others whose names I don't remember, people who were strangers for the most part. For reasons unknown to us, there were no more sauna adventures or parties at the prof's cabin home.

The rest of the term went well. I passed the first term classes with distinction and great distinction. Like the year before when we lived in Edmonton, we had made the decision to return to Wynyard for Christmas. Unlike the previous year we had more days available for visiting family.

Back in Nelson following the Christmas break, life soon settled into familiar patterns. Maksym soon joined us as originally planned. It was good for me to have him rejoin us. He was my best friend. The only drawback was the loss of privacy. Marynia worked at the bank while I attended classes and completed assignments, as the second term flowed into springtime. One of the projects was the creation of a chapbook of poetry which had earned high praise from my English professor. He predicted that I would someday make my mark as an author and poet.

With the approach of the end of the school year, I had learned that I would be able to begin an education program. Having gained the highest marks of his class, the future was open for whatever career path I wanted to follow according to the course counsellor. I then spent more than a few hours with the counsellor in order to explore the options. I had a goal in mind, a degree in education that would have a major in Native Studies. I had previously told Marynia that I was Métis, what some in our family called Ojihawk Métis – Ojibwe and Mohawk ancestry – to go along with my French and English roots.

"So, if I major in Native Studies, I would get a job teaching a lot easier than if I stuck to majoring in English and History," I explained in an attempt to convince Marynia.

"That's a great idea, Bob! But they don't have a program for Native Studies here, do they?"

"No. It seems that only the University of Saskatchewan and another university in Ontario offer Native Studies programs."

"So, that means that we'll have to move again," noted Marynia who was not looking forward to yet another move, especially as she had made a few friends at work. She loved where we lived. Having heard my rationale, she asked, "Have you decided which university you want to go to?"

"I thought maybe the one in Saskatoon," I offered. "It's close to your home and family. It will make it easier for both of us. What do you think?"

Marynia was thankful that I had chosen the University of Saskatchewan, though she had really wished we could stay in Nelson. After all, a teacher was a teacher and she was beginning to feel like a gypsy. Moving so often, had left her feeling that no place was home. Home had become a place left somewhere in the past. Still, she knew I was right about job prospects as a teacher. And above all, the future she wanted, needed the stability of my having a good career.

"That sounds okay, Bob," she said as she forced a note of cheer into her voice.

Near the end of the school year, Maksym had left a few weeks earlier to return to work in Edmonton. We finally had some private time as a couple. During our last week in

Nelson, we went for a final walk through the foothills of the mountains. Having taken a new path, we came across a house in one of the small valleys. The house was home to a commune of young people, who had chosen to embrace a different lifestyle. A young woman had seen us walking and invited us to join their group for a light lunch, a vegetarian lunch. Marynia was excited to try this new experience.

Once inside the large and airy house, we were invited to join the group for a pre-lunch meditation. Neither of us had tried meditation in the past, though we both knew a bit about meditation. Following the examples set by the others, we sat cross-legged on cushions set on the floor. With the sunlight pouring in through the numerous windows, we experienced our first meditation. Something shifted within me as I sat there, something vital was stirred within as I risked letting go of control.

Back at the apartment, I spoke to Marynia, "Wow! That was something else. I mean I knew about meditation, but actually trying it just blew my mind."

"It was okay," Marynia acknowledged, "but the food was incredible. Lentils, chickpeas, and sprouts ... I think I'll be adding a lot more vegetables to our diet. Not that I want us to become vegetarians, but it seemed to me to be a very healthy way to eat. Even their way of living. They reminded me, in a way, of a commune not far from the farm back home. It wasn't as nice as this one, but it makes me think that living more naturally would be well worth trying. What do you think, Bob?"

"I think I'd love to try living a lot more naturally. Of course, I still want to get my teaching license and a teaching job as well. It takes money to live naturally."

Two days after the final exam, we attended the awards ceremony. I had achieved the highest marks in several courses and had placed in the top ten overall for first year students. With a final standing of great distinction, my scholarship at the University of Saskatchewan was assured. Other awards included books and much praise. The most valued of all the kind words, were those spoken by my English professor who spoke of me as a poet and author in the making. And then, with the awards ceremony finished, we packed up our truck for the long journey to Wynyard and the family farm where we would live for the next three months until it was time to move to Saskatoon.

Chapter Three – University Life in Saskatoon

First and last photo of my siblings and mother, May 1973.

Marynia and I moved to Saskatoon, Saskatchewan in September 1973. I had registered in the College of Education, with a major in First Nation studies. Having earned a few scholarships at Nelson had proven I would be more than capable at succeeding.

I took on the challenges of the larger university and continued to excel with my studies. As was the case in Nelson, my peer group was made up of young professors and instructors, as well as a few older students. Like Icarus flying high, I was soon soaring with a swollen ego. Focusing on university life, I forgot all about caring for my body. I was so "self" focused, I wasn't paying enough attention to Marynia, leaving her almost abandoned while I was competing for honours, as though they were hunting trophies. Yet, at times, while sitting at my desk working on yet another term paper, I would turn to look at Marynia who was sitting quietly in the background. Seeing her, I remembered why I was trying so hard. This beautiful woman was the centre of my universe. And so, for a while, I became more attentive.

On those rare occasions, when seeing Marynia with eyes unfocused and with her head bowed, I would feel a wave of guilt wash over me. Marynia had never said anything, never complained, and would always put a smile on her face when I finally did speak to her. I knew that I was being selfish. Becoming a teacher was important for our future as a couple, and eventually as a family. However, that didn't mean that I had to steal more time from her than was necessary. My guilt was a Catholic guilt. I believed that in being a true and devoted husband, I would be more fully present with Marynia.

It was after seeing her sitting quietly one evening when I turned back to the work sitting on the desk. Setting the research paper to the side and taking out another piece of paper, I wrote:

The Philosopher and His Marynia

Taking for granted your need and your warmth
Taking for granted, tomorrow
I sit silently with a book in my hand
And I silently, so silently, leave you.

Gone to mountains of Philosophy and dead men
Gone in pursuit of the eternal
Nietzsche, Teilhard de Chardin, Spinoza, and Buddha
Beckon to the fringes of my mind.

Racing through the myths of other men's dreams
Racing through their pain and strife
My spirit soars in recognition of kinship
Then, seeing you, I fall back to earth.

You sit there painfully waiting for my return to you
Waiting for my return to the present hoping that I won't be
long

And you, so quiet, so sad, and so calm
You who I call my wife and best friend

You sit still waiting, looking for my eyes to see you
Hoping that I don't see you cry.

I drop my book and walk two million miles
Back to you and your essence grounded in reality
I walk back to hold you close and breath your essence
That tells me you are the only truth.

Turning back to look at Marynia, I got out of my chair and gave her the poem I had just written for her.

"Will you forgive me?" I asked while she read the poem, her tears now freely flowing.

"There's nothing to forgive, Bob. I understand that you need to work hard on your courses. I love you," she spoke as she clung to me. "I know that you have to do well, for us. I want you to know that I will always be here waiting for you when you have time for me."

~

Before the end of the second month of classes I had been given a contract to teach in the northern part of the province, at a school located in Camsell Portage. At an interview with the Northern Lights School Division held at the university in early October, I had asked the man who would become my future Director of Education, Ed Law, which school was the furthest north within the school division. My intention was to teach at that school. Several days later, Ed Law called and told me I was being offered a conditional contract to be the teaching principal of the two-room school in Camsell Portage, a tiny village just north east of Uranium City, Saskatchewan. Once I had a teacher's licence in hand, the conditional contract would be finalised.

Marynia and I socialised with my Educational Foundations professor, Ben and his wife, Sophia. Ben had persuaded Marynia and me to register for Transcendental Meditation classes. Sophia was an artist who encouraged Marynia to develop her artistic side through macramé. As well as Ben and Sophia, we socialised with Ed Law and his girlfriend Jane. Having other people in our lives helped both of us weather the isolation of living in a city. As well, it gave Marynia a break from being alone. She was a people person and needed more human interaction.

With the pressure to find a teaching job resolved, Marynia and I were both excited and motivated. All I had to do at this point, was to focus on passing the classes to ensure getting a teaching certificate. Because of our savings while at Nelson, due in most part to Marynia's job at the bank; as well as another student loan, and a scholarship that paid for my tuition: money wasn't an issue. We had rented a nice home on Main Street well within our budget. The garden on the farm had provided us with a lot of our food, as had wild meat from Marynia's hunting brothers.

Having recently bought a new camera, a single-lens-reflex camera, I had taken a more serious interest in photography in Saskatoon. I had set up a darkroom in the basement of the house on Main Street. Marynia was frequently the subject in the photos. I was determined to somehow capture the magic she radiated, in the photos. She was my magical other, the holder of my soul.

The fall and winter passed quickly, and it was time for the final practicum, a month of teaching on the James Smith Reserve, near Kinistino. The reserve was about an hour east of Prince Albert. Marynia spent the month with me on the reserve. The four weeks were marked with the freedom to experiment with teaching strategies. I had been given the opportunity to do what I thought best with my assigned classes. It wasn't long before I earned enough trust to teach them unsupervised.

Life on the reserve was a mixture of chaos and exuberance. Because of inclement weather near the end of the internship, the school closed for a few days bringing my practicum to an end. I was given the highest rating possible by the University supervisor and my school supervisor. I now had a Standard "A" teaching certificate. I had officially become a teacher. Returning to Saskatoon and contacting Ed, the Director of Education, I received confirmation as teaching-principal for the school in Camsell Portage in April 1974.

After registering for an intersession class, and a summer class, Marynia and I flew off to Ottawa to surprise my mother with a Mother's Day visit. It was an idea that Marynia had suggested. My parents had finally divorced. My mother had relocated from the acreage, to a low-rent townhouse in the city. She seemed to be happier than I could remember her being for a long time. My brothers and sisters were also happier with one exception: the new man who had entered their life. He was a brutal man who instilled fear in my siblings.

My sister Béatrice had married a young man named Mark. Mark was a photographer and a technician in the CBC film industry and had several reels of unused 35mm stored in his freezer. When he found out about my interest in photography, he gave me two reels of the film. I now didn't have to worry about photography eating up so much of our limited resources.

Laurent, my father, made an appearance, giving us a late wedding gift of a ginger-bread clock that unsurprisingly didn't work. For the hour he was present, there was a pretense by everyone that everything was normal. When Laurent finally left, I captured a final image of my siblings and my mother. It was the first and last image of all of us nine siblings. For some reason, I didn't want this photo to include my father.

With a teaching contract in place, Marynia and I conceived our first child while in Ottawa on the Mother's Day weekend. Then, we returned to Saskatoon. We began to plan the move to Camsell Portage. Whatever we bought, mostly dry, bulk food items, would have to be shipped by train to Fort Chipewyan, and then by barge to the village of Camsell Portage, the most northerly point of Lake Athabasca, only 45 kilometres south of the Northwest Territories border.

Though we were excited about the move to Camsell Portage, knowing we had conceived a child was infinitely more exciting. I took photos of Marynia to document the visible evidence that the passing months presented of our baby growing within her. Unfortunately, Marynia was often nauseated during those first few months but didn't let that allow her to be anything but happy. Life seemed to be perfect. I had a job, we were going to be parents, and the future belonged to us.

I decided to take a summer class to learn the Cree language as part of moving towards getting a professional teaching certificate, which required a full Bachelor of Education degree. I assumed that the language would also make my teaching in an indigenous community that much easier. Marynia kept herself busy with gardening and other projects while I was in classes. A new chapter in our lives was about to begin.

Chapter Four – Camsell Portage and Fatherhood

The christening of Nola, our first child, in Camsell Portage, 1975.

At the end of August 1974, Marynia and I moved into the tiny village of Camsell Portage, the northernmost community in the province. There were no roads to Camsell Portage, nor any vehicles in the village, other than boats and snow machines. Camsell Portage was a remote, fly-in community. There wasn't even a store in the village. Barges would dock in order to bring in bulk supplies, such as fuel and building supplies. I had our supplies sent by barge from Fort Chipewyan, Alberta. Our arrival in the community was made via a small Cessna float plane taken from Uranium City. Our arrival at the dock was witnessed by most of the village children and a few interested adults.

The community was at the northwestern end of a bay off the northern edge of Lake Athabasca. The teacherage was just off the shore of the bay, a relatively modern bungalow with two bedrooms. A sand-point well provided crystal-clear drinking water. Marynia fell in love with her new home.

The village was a mixture of Treaty and Métis people, except for a visiting priest and a man from France. He had married a local woman, the leading lady of the community who was to be my teaching assistant. I taught, hunted, worked on photographs, wrote, and hiked through the hills with Marynia. When we hiked, we often had a collection of youth trailing after us. With life filled to overflowing, meditation which had begun less than a year earlier, had faded into the past. Life became fully lived in the present.

Marynia quickly became best friends with Mary, the wife of a man from France called Philippe. Their family lived in a large, beautiful, log home. We were frequent visitors to their home. It was inevitable that we would become very close. It was the first time in my life that I had become this close to others who weren't in my or Marynia's extended family. The closeness of classmates and university professors I had adopted as friends, were always kept at a safe distance. Being accepted simply as me, husband of Marynia and as the community teacher, filled a hole within me that I hadn't been aware even existed.

Life was constantly providing new experiences in the north country. Fishing, hunting, berry picking, and simply walking forest trails, filled the early autumn months. The occasional air flight into Uranium City for groceries, as well as travelling to Uranium once on Philippe's commercial fishing boat, were the only occasions when we were absent from the village. The only access to the village was either by plane, or by boat. I began to consciously fully embrace life, being present in the world outside of home and my relationship to Marynia. I knew that this was living a life with meaning.

Marynia and I returned to Saskatoon for a teachers' convention, and then went on to Wynyard for the remainder of the October long weekend of 1974 where we attended the marriage of Maksym. When we returned to Camsell Portage, we didn't have much time to enjoy autumn, as it soon turned to winter. My life as teacher and principal was all that I had hoped for, and more. For Marynia, the nausea of her early pregnancy had retreated, and she became more involved with community life. There were no regrets by either of us about our decision to choose Camsell Portage as home.

A second trip out of the community was taken at Christmas time. We picked up our truck, which had been parked at her brother's place in Saskatoon, then drove to Wynyard. With holidays coming to an end, we returned to Camsell Portage in early January 1975. Then, back at home, in the early morning hours of January 7th, Marynia went into labour.

"Bob!" Marynia called out as she lay in bed just after seven in the morning while I was at my desk preparing lessons. "I think I'm going into labour. You'd better call for a plane to take us to Uranium."

I was surprised as the baby wasn't due for another month. Yet, not doubting her concern, I called out, "I'll go to Mary's first, she's expecting to go with us when we go in for the baby's delivery It's a bit early, are you sure that this isn't false labour?"

The two of us had been studying a small handful of books about home delivery in case isolation became an issue. I was ready, but I really hoped that the baby would be born in a hospital. The last thing I wanted to do was to make a mistake during the baby's delivery and cause it harm.

"It's the real thing, Bob," Marynia stated emphatically. "You'll have to hurry."

I got my winter gear on, as it was minus 37 Celsius. As promised, I went to Mary's house first, in order to have her go back to our place to check on Marynia.

"She's dilating," declared Mary. "She is definitely going to have her baby today, or tomorrow at the latest. Go order the plane, Bob!"

The weather was so cold that I was unable to get a Cessna or a Beaver airplane, either of the planes that normally would be taken to get to Uranium City. Finally, after a delay, I got called back. They would have to use a larger plane, an Otter, as it was the only plane that would start. The plane arrived a short while later and the three of us: Marynia, Mary, and I got on the plane. Once we landed in Uranium not many minutes later, I rushed Marynia to the hospital in a taxi. Mary said she would go to the hospital later, as she was first heading into town for a bit of shopping.

"Since it's your first baby," Mary informed Marynia, "It will be a few more hours before the baby will arrive. I'll go to the hospital just after lunch. Don't worry, I'll be there when your baby is born."

"But Mary, the baby is almost here, I know it. Noon will be too late," Marynia told her best friend.

"Don't worry, I'll be there when you deliver your baby. I promise." Mary had given birth to five children and understood that first-time mothers always were in a panic. Usually, the waiting stretched on for hours and hours.

Marynia and I arrived at the hospital just after ten in the morning. Marynia was immediately taken to the delivery room while I filled in the needed paperwork. Then, following the nurse, I rushed into the delivery room holding my camera. Together, Marynia and I had agreed to record the birth in photos for our private memories, photos that would complete the record of our baby's growth we had begun back in Saskatoon when Marynia knew she had become pregnant. Almost as soon as I arrived in the delivery room, the doctor told Marynia she could start pushing.

I jumped between comforting Marynia and taking photos of the birth. The doctor suggested various photo angles during the delivery. And then, a baby girl emerged. Marynia and I had names already picked out ahead of time. The camera had been set aside while I held my tiny daughter Nola, who was now wrapped in a miniature blanket.

"Hello there, princess. Papa is here," I spoke to the small baby, smaller than I had expected. She had arrived almost a month early and I began to worry, unnecessarily. She was beautiful, but so small that my heart ached with both pride and fear.

"She's hungry," Marynia stated as she held out her arms to take back her baby. "We did it, Bob. We created a bit of perfection in this world." Turning to Nola, Marynia added, "Hey there, Nola. Mom has some milk for you. Come and try it, breakfast is ready."

With the birth of our daughter Nola, we became even closer, if that could have even been possible. Parenting quickly became a shared role for both of us. Since I had more experience with babies and child care, as the eldest child in my family, I shared what I knew, mostly by example. Most of my intellectual projects were set aside so I could be more present with my tiny family. I was filled to the brim with the roles of teacher, principal, friend, husband, and now, father.

In the spring, the excitement of a planned trip to the south with the senior students accelerated. Money had been raised with movie nights at the school, bingos at the school, and even a bake sale. It was to be the final event of the school year, just after the last day of classes. The school year had been shortened with the addition of more teaching time during each day of classes, as an attempt to improve attendance. With spring breakup and the commencement of the commercial fishing season, attendance at the school had traditionally been less than half. It had been my idea to solve the problem fewer students following spring break-up.

The trip went off without any issue. When the students returned home, it was time for me and Marynia to return to the farm, where we would spend the summer introducing Nola to the extended family. We left with the expectation of returning to a place we had begun to envision as perhaps our permanent home. We had even picked out the site where we would build our own log home.

Chapter Five – Ile-a-la-Crosse

A coureur de bois at heart on Lake Athabasca,
a peek at an inner wildness man, 1975.

In October 1975, I was transferred out of Camsell Portage following the annual teachers' convention in Saskatoon. I didn't know it at the time, but in the background, I had negatively affected my chances of remaining in the community. I hadn't given Mary her due as a powerful voice in the community. I assumed that as principal, I didn't always need permission or approval, other than from Ed Law, the Director. With the new school year, I had begun to make decisions without discussing them first with Mary. It was the first sign of an issue that would plague me for decades, an issue with the power of the feminine, or put in psychological terms, a mother-complex. In addition, I suffered from hubris. I saw myself as better than most people when it came to education and teaching, especially teacher assistants.

We were moved to Ile-a-la-Crosse, a Métis community closer to the centre of the province. I had been loaned to the school for the year by the Director, to fill a high-school position. The teacher had quit during the October convention. I soon found myself in teacher heaven, working with high school students. I didn't know it at the time, but the new position was the best thing that could have happened to me. Because of my new-found passion as a high school teacher, I resonated with the students as much as my teaching assignment resonated with me.

I had persuaded the senior students to adapt a Métis play, *The Ecstasy of Rita Joe*, for public performance. They worked hard at adapting portions of the script to reflect their own lives and community. They worked even harder to bring the play to life through their acting. When the play was performed, my status as a writer was acknowledged by the community. I poured heart and soul into teaching. I took small field trips with the younger students to have them write in various locations, hoping that nature and their community's history would inspire them as writers.

Still unconscious of community dynamics working in the background, I hadn't realised that a teacher is always under a microscope within a community. In Camsell Portage that lack of awareness resulted in my being transferred. Even though I wasn't a principal anymore, I was noticed and evaluated by the community on an almost daily basis. The students took stories of what happened at school to their homes. The adults of the community were aware of Marynia and me when we walked around the town. Unlike most of the teachers who drove everywhere, we were visible and present in the community. We had brought our truck to Ile-a-la-Crosse. Yet, regardless of having the truck there, we continued to walk everywhere in town, only using the truck when we ventured out of town.

Because of what the community had learned about me, I had been asked to write the town's bicentennial history book soon after the Christmas break. The community was going to celebrate its bicentennial and wanted a book included as part of the bicentennial projects. Marynia was ecstatic that her husband was finally being recognised as a writer. Accepting the challenge, I wasted no time in going through the community records, including the photos stored in the old hospital and neighbouring convent. The book needed to be well researched. Two hundred years of the community's history was a story that needed to be told. With the Internet not yet invented, the research took me to the provincial archives in Saskatoon. I had found enough information by the beginning of March to have a pamphlet designed advertising the late winter games, with the book to follow when it was completed.

The book project kept me busy, perhaps too busy for Marynia and Nola. Even when I was at home, I seemed to talk only about the book. With the blessing and support of the Bicentennial Committee, I booked a plane flight to Ottawa for Marynia, Nola and me. There was more research still to do.

All the expenses for researching and producing the materials for the book, including travel expenses, were being paid for by the Bicentennial Committee, chaired by the community's mayor. I paid for Marynia's and Nola's tickets. Our time spent in Ottawa was pleasant, with visits to a few aunts and uncles, as well as my French grandparents, when I wasn't spending time at the National Library Archives.

My mother had given up the abusive partner she had paired up with following her divorce. She had met another man, Jack. My mother was happy. It was a relief that was reflected in my siblings. That relief was noticed by Marynia. We left Ottawa with the last of the needed material for the book, and with a good feeling about my family in Ottawa.

When we got back to Ile-a-la-Crosse, we decided it was time to have a sibling for Nola. The book was nearing completion. There would be a new school back under the directorship of Ed, in the Northern Lights School Division. And best of all, for Marynia, she saw I was finally succeeding as a teacher in a northern community. It was going to be a new beginning for us as a family.

Once back in Ile-a-la-Crosse, I gathered as much local information as I could, using my senior students to help gather stories from the elders. I was given five thousand dollars for the completed book, more money than I earned for a year of teaching. The windfall and the knowledge that I would be guaranteed another teaching job, caused the two to celebrate. Another baby was planned for and conceived.

By the beginning of June, the Director took us to check out a school in Sturgeon Landing, another two-room school. I was offered the role of teaching principal. The house was the best we had yet seen, almost new. The community was picturesque. There was a small river burbling in the background behind the house. Best of all, we weren't far from a city, the city of The Pas, Manitoba. We needed that security, as our second child would likely be born there. We returned to Ile-a-la-Crosse to finish the school year. There was only a short time left for me to gather everything needed before I could begin writing the book, so the research and preliminary writing efforts increased.

As the end of the school year approached, my senior class asked if they could have a graduation event. This was the first grade eleven class at the school in the recent history and they wanted to mark it as a significant event. The principal was quick to give his permission making me the person in charge of making the event happen. The students wanted a banquet in the community centre and so the work began with a student committee of girls working to put the pieces together: the meal, the music, the guests, and the decorations. My role was to get the necessary clearances from the community and the school.

With the event set for the last day of school, I couldn't find any teachers willing to chaperone the dance at the school to follow the banquet. Some teachers were set on leaving the community before the event, and others were worried about having to deal with drunken and stoned students and community adults. Horror stories were brought out to justify their unwillingness to help. As the day approached, the only person I had as a chaperone was Marynia. I began to dread what would likely happen with no adults to supervise the post-banquet dance being held at the school.

The banquet went off without a hitch, with parents and students and assorted extended family all in attendance and helping out as best they could. All Marynia and I had to do was to be present and smile for the most part.

I was sitting outside of the school, waiting for the last of the decorations to be set up for the dance, as well as to cool off from the heat of the late afternoon. One of the students came to me with a look of concern.

"Mr. Robert, TJ's coming. He's going to trash our dance. We have to do something," he pleaded, believing that I would be able to fix this.

TJ was a big man, a Métis who had put a few RCMP officers in the hospital and had earned time in the provincial jail system as a result. I was a small, young man who didn't and couldn't fight. There had been rumours that TJ wanted to hurt me for not including him as a resource person for the community history book. As I saw TJ approaching, with a case of beer tucked under each arm, I had a thought.

"TJ," I called out knowing that TJ was intent on entering the school just as the students were preparing it for the dance. "I've been told that a number of guys are intending to trash the students' grad dance. Can I get you to be our bouncer and keep them out, so they don't ruin the grad dance?"

Grinning, TJ set the cases of beer beside the entrance of the school and took a seat beside me. "Damn rights I'll be your bouncer. There's no way them assholes are gonna wreck tonight for the kids. Damn straight of you to be on the kids' side with getting them this grad. Only one condition though," TJ spoke with a serious look that looked more than a bit dangerous to me.

"What's that?" I asked hesitantly.

"You gotta have a toke with me. I got me some of the finest weed in the north."

TJ went with me into the school. I convinced him to put the cases of beer in the staff room. TJ stood by the gym door, an imposing figure who frightened anyone who may have thought to become a problem at the dance. A few teachers showed up at the dance to make an appearance. In the end, a few of them agreed to spell the parents who had been helping supervise the dance. When the last of the students left, and after helping with the cleanup of the gym, the school year was officially over.

The school year was done. We packed our belongings into the back of the half ton truck. It was time to move back to the farm outside of Wynyard, our summer home.

Chapter Six – Sturgeon Landing Challenges and a Second Child

Natalie, our second child at home in Sturgeon Landing, 1977.

We returned to the farm, and the cottage that Marynia called the bunkhouse. Nola was the centre of attraction for her brother Wasyl's two children, Charlotte and Travis. They were quick to include Nola, now one-and-a-half, in games of dress-up, or whatever other suitable activity they came up with. It was a summer of relaxation. I spent some of my time trying to improve the cottage by building extra cupboards. The expectation was that we would be more than welcome to stay in the "bunkhouse" for a few years until we had a place of our own. The work seemed worthwhile.

Summer passed very quickly, and soon we were moving our belongings, including the extra pieces of furniture that had been stored on the farm since we had left Saskatoon. It took two trips to move everything to Sturgeon Landing at the end of August 1976.

The difference between Camsell Portage and Sturgeon Landing had everything to do with the presence of the First Nations Reserve on the other side of the river, and the access to the community by road. In addition, there was a store and fishing lodge in the village. The store and resort were owned and operated by a couple who were Caucasian. There were two young women from Québec working for the season at the store and lodge. They soon became Marynia's friends. Having already lived and worked in northern communities, we both were accepted by the people of the community. Unknown to both Marynia and I, was the violent history of the community.

I had learned from my mistakes in Camsell Portage and didn't push as hard when working with my new teacher assistant, Kathy, and the caretaker, Leonard. My focus was spent on making classes more interesting in hopes of encouraging the students to come and stay in school. The attendance rate for the school had been abysmal in the past, with often more than half the students missing. Focusing on making their experience at school positive, became the key in having most of the students return to attending classes. A few unannounced visits by the Director resulted in nore praise for me.

Marynia soon developed a level of trust with Kathy, who became Nola's baby sitter on the rare occasions when one was needed. Nola liked Kathy and would often spend time in the primary classroom looking at picture books, even when school was in session. Also falling in love with little Nola, was an old trapper from southern Saskatchewan, Medric

Poirier, and his niece Marguerite, who lived in one of the village houses.

When not in classes, Marynia and I would take Nola on small hikes, taking a picnic lunch to enjoy along the river, watching beavers working on building a beaver lodge. It was an early autumn, and it was a northland paradise.

But then it all changed. The Director had flown in to Sturgeon Landing to take me to a principals' conference in La Ronge. Marynia had asked Annette, one of the girls working at the store, to stay at the house while I was gone for two nights. Not aware that anyone was in the house, the caretaker, Leonard decided to enter and help himself to a few things, mostly from the fridge and pantry. When Annette heard noise and saw the outline of someone on the back porch, she screamed. Leonard took off without getting what he wanted, and Marynia woke to Annette's scream. Annette told Marynia about what she had seen. The two young women decided that they couldn't possibly go back asleep. Together, they sat in the kitchen with all the lights in the house turned on, waiting for morning.

When I arrived home just before noon the next day, Marynia told me in no uncertain terms, "You've got to tell Ed, there's no way that you're ever going to a conference or meeting again if we don't get to travel and stay with you. Bob. We can't raise our children here. Ed needs to find you another school, in a safer community." Marynia vented her fear and frustration, which had turned into anger. I had left her and Nola alone, unprotected and vulnerable.

The Director knew that Marynia wouldn't change her mind, when I told him about Marynia's demands. Ed promised to make sure that the school division covered her travel and living expenses, as it had covered mine. Ed didn't want to lose me as a teaching principal. He had plans for me to eventually be a principal in a larger school, once I had more experience.

For the rest of the autumn, things went well, with only one event that troubled us. On Halloween evening, the younger students had collected their treats. Helping Marynia pass out the treats, was a nurse named Marlene, who was staying at the health centre with her adult daughter, Jessica. It was a warm evening, and everyone was enjoying the small procession of children who came to the door. Later in the evening, with the younger children indoors; the older youth took to pulling the school fence across the only road through the village, just one of the numerous pranks in the community.

Since I was worried about keeping the road open in case an ambulance was needed, I went outside to repeatedly move the fence off the road. No sooner had I returned to the house, when the youth would reappear to pull it back onto the road. The game went on and on for some time.

Finally, I had had enough. Taking my rifle out, I sighted the barrel to discharge above the faint treeline to the east, then pulled the trigger. The youth fled, and the night became very silent in response. Halloween was over.

The next morning, Marlene came over to tell her story about how some crazy man was shooting late in the evening. She spoke of how she immediately had dropped to the floor and hid under the bed assuming the natives would continue firing weapons. Marynia and I never told her that I was the one who had fired the shot, or why I had done so.

The rest of the First Nations' community knew who had fired the shot; the crazy Frenchman, the school teacher. In a way I would never have expected, this touch of craziness resulted in my gaining a strange level of respect. When I tried to introduce native crafts into the school curriculum for my students weeks later, the elders were more than willing to teach the adolescent youth how to do beadwork, how to make snowshoes, and how to work with wood according to age-old traditions. The crazy Frenchman had earned respect, as a man touched by the gods.

During the fall, I had finished writing out the manuscript for the Ile-a-la-Crosse Bicentennial book, with Marynia typing the longhand notes into book form. The finished document was sent off to the printing company. Before long, the proofs were mailed back for corrections. It wasn't long after the Christmas holidays, when the book was finally printed.

When we returned from the Christmas break spent in Wynyard, we found out that someone had broken into the house while we were gone. We were both upset and angry. Carefully checking through our belongings, all that appeared to be missing were a few blankets and a jar of peanut butter. Someone broke in because of need, not to rob them. Nothing of importance had been taken, nothing had been destroyed. Regardless, the damage to our confidence had been done. Sturgeon Landing didn't feel like a good place to raise a family.

Then, as with Nola's birth, the time for Marynia's labour had begun. Like with our first child, time was of the essence. The winter road had been maintained, so there was little time wasted as I drove Marynia to the hospital in The Pas. Nola was left in the care of Kathy. And, as I had with Nola's birth, I closed the school with the Director's permission. Natalie was born on time, unlike her older sister.

A few weeks after Natalie was brought home, the RCMP sergeant from Cumberland House had arrived to provide a brief police presence in the community. Life in the community and the neighbouring reserve were becoming increasingly unsettled. Marynia invited the sergeant to stay for supper and for the night. We had an extra guest room expressly for the purpose of such guests, and with the expectation that we offered its use. The sergeant was enjoying supper with us, when a group of angry locals arrived at the house demanding that I send out the sergeant. I knew that the men were under the influence of alcohol, and I had no doubts about what would happen to the sergeant should he go out to face the men.

"I'll go talk to them," I told the sergeant. "While I'm doing that, you go out by the back door and get to safety."

"Are you crazy?" Marynia shouted. "They have rifles. You have two little girls, Bob. What am I going to do if they shoot you?" she added in panic with tears running down her face.

"They won't shoot me," I stated as if it was an obvious fact. "Remember, I'm the crazy teacher. They respect crazy men, they think we are touched by the gods."

With that, I ignored Marynia's tears and pleas for sanity, and went to the front door. I opened the door and stepped out to talk with the eight men who had gathered in front of the house. They were intoxicated as I had expected; and, five of them had rifles.

"We don't want you, crazy man," one of the men spoke in protest. "We want the sergeant."

"Well, he can't come out to meet you guys," I stated, ignoring the threat of violence that hung thick in the air. "The truth is, the Sergeant isn't here anymore."

"Liar! We saw him go in earlier."

"Well, he's not in my house any more. You're too late. He told me he had to get back to Cumberland House. He left right after he ate with us."

The men looked at each other, then at me. Since I knew that the sergeant had already left the house, I was able to talk to the men without lying to them. They knew I didn't lie. Those touched by the gods didn't lie. "Crazy fucker! You send a message to the Sergeant that he'd better not come back, or we'll bury him here."

Having requested a new school, I was given just one option, as an elementary teacher in Buffalo Narrows, for the next school year. It was either that or to remain in Sturgeon Landing. Buffalo Narrows was a community not too far from Ile-a-la-Crosse. It was a large school, and as far as both Marynia and I were concerned, a safer place to raise two girls. Talking with both the principal and vice-principal of the school, both of whom had young children and lived in the community, Marynia agreed to the relocation destination.

She knew she would have to settle in a new home again. However, the only other option was to remain in Sturgeon Landing, a choice she was adamantly against. It seemed that since she had met me, all she did was move. She knew that her family needed to have roots. Perhaps Buffalo Narrows, and the teacherage next to the principal and vice-principal would finally be the place she could call home.

Chapter Seven – Buffalo Narrows and a Return to University

A return to nature between university classes 1978.

Marynia's brother Wasyl, who owned the family homestead, had built a new home on a quarter of land not far from the old farm house. Marynia and I now had the old farmhouse to ourselves for the summer of 1977. We moved the stored items from the cottage, into the old house. It was the first time we had the old farmyard and house to ourselves. It was a feeling that I revelled in. Marynia could sense how I finally felt at ease. She saw me smile for what appeared to be no reason other than being together as a family. There were no distractions, no need to focus on others and trying to please them.

It wasn't long before Wasyl invited us over for a meal at his new home, which was about three kilometres away from the old house.

"You two seem to love that old house," Wasyl began, as we sat at the table. "What do you think about buying the old home quarter? It seems no one else in the family is interested in buying the place. That said, we all agree that the home quarter has to stay in the family."

I turned to look at Marynia with a hopeful look. She smiled as she looked at her brother, "That depends," she answered. "How much would it cost, and just what would we be buying?"

Over the next few weeks, those answers were hashed out with the result being a trip to a lawyer. We now officially owned a small quarter section of land, mostly rolling and treed hills, with about fifty acres of crop land, and the old farmyard and its buildings with contents. The money from the book, as well as our savings from three years of teaching in the north, meant that we would own the property outright leaving no debt. We bought the farm. It was the first time I had ever lived in a home that belonged to me or my family. I had grown up in poverty, constantly moving from place to place whenever my father had fallen behind in rent.

-

A week after we moved into our new home in Buffalo Narrows, young Garnet Stelle from Camsell Portage moved in to live with us. He was intent on getting more education having finished his last grade in the two-room school in Camsell Portage. The Stelle family trusted us enough to consider us as a host family for their son. It was a good arrangement for all of us. Contact with the Stelle family had been maintained even though distance separated us. After all, Mary and Philippe were Nola's godparents.

Life at home, with two neighbouring families, with whom we became very close friends, was the best it had been since they had travelled to the north for my teaching career. However, teaching had become more of a job than a passion. Yet, with the frequent escapes into nature to fish, hike, and take photographs, I was happy none-the-less. It wasn't long before we made even more friends, including people who were not teachers. Marynia began to think that we would be living in this home for the long term, at least until we were ready to move back to the farm for good.

Fall turned to winter and life continued to be good. Winter turned to spring, and with that shift, we unexpectedly learned that both the principal and vice-principal would be leaving the school to work as principals in the southern school system closer to Prince Albert. Marynia was saddened to see her best friends leave, as the stay-at-home mothers and their children would be gone by the end of the school year.

Since housing was assigned by the principal, Marynia learned that there was no guarantee that she would even be able remain in the house we now called home. I began to experience increasing back pain that I blamed on an old injury. However, it was really a physical response to the mental pressures that were building within me.

With the news of the principal and vice-principal leaving in June, the jockeying among the staff to see who would become the school administrators, became intense. As the best friend of the outgoing administration, I was locked out of the conversations that were often heated. In early May, I was showing cracks in my confidence as a teacher and as a person. I knew that I would never have more than an outsider role, if I was even able to remain in the school. My doubts about my teaching future consumed me. I began running again to escape the depression that began to arise from self-doubts. I didn't know what I was running from, but I did know that it wasn't about some concern over my physical fitness.

"Bob!" Marynia called out to me as I had ignored her earlier question. "What's the matter with you? Why aren't you talking to me anymore?"

"I'm sorry," I apologised, though not sure why I was apologising.

"What's the matter with you? You look like living with me is torture. Talk to me!"

I didn't know what to say, but knew I had to say something. "I'm not sure I'll have a job here next year. Sheila will be the next principal with Don being her vice-principal. The word is out that our house will be given to Sheila's best friend, April. Sheila has arranged meetings with most of the teachers about next year's teaching assignments, but not with me."

"So why not resign?" Marynia stated as if it was the obvious solution. "We've already talked about you finishing your teaching degree. We could go to Saskatoon and you can take the classes you still need. With a degree, you'll be able to get a job in a southern school where we can settle down. You'll never get a job in the Wynyard area all that easily without a degree."

Hearing the news of my returning to study at the university for the next school year, our friends and neighbours were quick to congratulate us. With any luck, and with their unconditional recommendations and references, they thought I would get a principal position in the rural areas near Prince Albert when I finished my degree. Then we would all live near each other in that city.

Once I had registered for classes, we drove to Saskatoon from Buffalo Narrows. We needed to find a place to live. We had a list of possible rentals which we found in the Saskatoon newspaper. It didn't take long to decide on a duplex within cycling distance of the university. We moved in to the rental a few days before I was to begin six weeks of summer classes. Though we had purchased the farm only the summer before, we would only get to go out to the farm once the summer session of classes ended, except for occasional weekends.

As in the past, I earned high marks in the two classes I took, which included a Fine Arts photography course. With the start of the regular university year, I found myself taking a class load of six classes. I had even less time to be present at home. The rationale was to finish the education degree in fourteen months time. We moved to another duplex at the end of summer session, this time only a block away from another of Marynia's brothers. It allowed Marynia to have the needed connections with family.

The months slipped passed, and winter turned into spring. It was time for me to take care of the business of finding a teaching job for the fall of 1979. I had been guaranteed a job in the Northern Lights School Division. I was offered the teaching-principalship at Timber Bay, a four-room school in the central north-central area of the province. An advertisement which Marynia had found in the newspaper, had me also apply for the vice-principal position at Blaine Lake, a significantly larger school in the central part of the province. That school appealed since we had begun to think ahead to when our girls would be attending school.

Marynia's father died during the Easter Week while I was writing final exams. A day after the news of her father's death, Marynia had found a teaching position advertised for in Lanigan, a community not far from Wynyard. She asked me to apply for the job so that our girls would get to interact more with their Ukrainian grandmother. The only problem with that job, it was for a French teacher in the high school. As well, the job interview at Blaine Lake had happened and I had been offered the job as vice-principal. I had a week to make a final decision.

"Bob, I don't want our girls to miss out on knowing their grandmother, my Mom. Your mom and dad are so far away, they are almost strangers to the girls. I don't want that to be the case with my Mom for the girls, especially since Dad is now gone."

I knew that she was right, Marynia's mother would only be three-quarters of an hour away if I took the job in Lanigan. My own mother and father were in Ottawa, too far away to be a real part of our girl's lives as grandparents. Though I had misgivings about getting the job because of the requirement of being a French teacher, I agreed.

"Okay, Marynia. Let's see if I can get the job."

Though I had a French-Canadian heritage, I had not studied any French since grade ten. Despite that fact, I was offered the position to teach French and other subjects at Lanigan Central High School. I hadn't expected the job offer and found myself conflicted. I had majored in First Nations Studies, yet I wanted a school where my daughters would be better able to fit in. Blaine Lake had seemed to be the best choice with both a Caucasian and First Nations presence. But with the death of Marynia's father, all that had changed. So, I declined the Blaine Lake job and accepted the position at Lanigan.

I changed my class for intersession and registered for a French immersion class in its place. For the first time since beginning university studies, I was unsure of being able to pass the course. How was I going to be able to succeed with a university level course in French when I had no formal education in French since early high school?

I was one of only a few immersion students who got to leave at the end of every class day. The others had to live in residence, where they continued to be immersed in the language. Yet, as the weeks passed, I began to gain confidence. The other students wondered why I was in the class with them since they thought I was much better at the language than them. Though they knew more about the structure and grammar, I sounded like a Francophone. My childhood in Ottawa, surrounded by a French-speaking family, had given me an intuitive base about the language the other students didn't have. I knew I would need to continue with some serious study of the language if I had any hopes of ever teaching French with any success.

With the job at Lanigan Central High School guaranteed, we began looking for a home in Lanigan. Marynia wanted a real home, a home we would own. The idea of eventually moving to live on the farm near Wynyard had been discarded. Marynia wanted distance from the town of Wynyard, distance from her past. There weren't a lot of options for homes when we visited the real estate office. We did find a place on an acreage just outside of town, but we weren't able to purchase the place before someone else had bought it.

The problem was we didn't have a down payment for a house. We knew we had to sell the family home quarter to get a down payment. It took until almost the end of June before the money from the sale of the homestead came in, allowing us to finally make an offer on a house on the eastern side of the town. The offer was accepted.

With a professional teacher's certificate and a degree in Education, a new home, and a shift in my career as a teacher, a new chapter had begun in my life. And as in the past when significant events appeared to make our future together better, we planned for and conceived our third child.

Part Two

Cracks Appearing in the Psyche

"Everything, everything, seems to ride on this thing called love. We love nature, we make love, we fall into and out of it, we pursue love and ask it to save us."

James Hollis – The Eden Project

The story of love and marriage has led to a place called home, a place of safety and peace where one finally relaxes and lets one guard down. And taking advantage of the cracks in the wall protecting the psyche, the dark shadows of the past begin to emerge.

Chapter Eight – The Past Rears It's Ugly Head

Dorian comes to us in Lanigan in the spring of 1980.

In the middle of August, we moved into our new home. It wasn't long before we made the acquaintances of our neighbours on the block. Across the street was a woman who taught in the high school, and two doors down was a man who taught in the elementary school. Almost every house on the street had young children.

For Marynia, almost as important as building community friendships, was the garden in which she had begun to invest her time and energy. She was determined to have it ready for the next gardening season.

I felt the pressure, a good pressure, in having to get ready to teach new courses in a new school. The teaching course load included French, History, and English. Used to working under pressure, after spending fourteen months at the university taking more than a normal class load, I quickly adapted to the routines that were part of being a teacher in a southern school, a White prairie school. That was how I defined it. I knew myself as an outsider, a French Canadian and an Easterner with indigenous heritage in a community that appeared to have no value for easterners, French-Canadians, or indigenous people. Time would teach me otherwise, especially as the community got to know me. However, I didn't know that at the time.

The weekend before classes were to begin, my father, Laurent, and his new wife, Deborah, arrived at our new home. Aside from my father smoking in the house, despite Marynia's request to keep the house smoke-free for the girls, the visit began well. I took my father to see the Métis site at Batoche. It was a rare time for us together. It was unlike anything I had remembered from the past. Rather than being a dominating presence, my father treated me as an equal. That afternoon showed me a new side of him. Despite the past when my father consistently denied any indigenous heritage, being Métis was acknowledged.

On our way back home, my father asked for some money to deal with a transmission problem with his car. Alarm bells began to ring loud for me. I realised that the visit had little, or nothing, to do with establishing a new relationship built on respect. Rather, it was the past come to life with my father trying once again, to get money from me.

When I told Marynia about Laurent's asking for money, she was quick to say, "No, Bob, we aren't rich. We just bought a home and we now have a huge debt, along with your student loan debt. We have two girls to raise and another child on the way. There's no way he's getting any money from us."

"You're right, Marynia," I knew she was right.

But in the end, I gave him some money, not the amount he had asked for, but too much regardless. It created a new rift between Marynia and me. Laurent and Deborah left, but what they left behind were the seeds of a shadow that would grow to consume me and my marriage. While I watched my father pull away, it dawned on me that my father had said nothing about my accomplishments at university, in my successfully getting a university degree, or more importantly, showing pride in being a grandfather to two incredible girls.

Despite the breach of trust between us that arose with giving my father some money, Marynia focused on her children. I had put my father first. Now, she would do her best to make sure that she wouldn't ever again be placed on the back burner because of my dysfunctional family background. She had children to care for and protect.

The staff was quick to welcome me to their team. As a result, the school year began on a positive note. And, as it had been previously, my passion for teaching pushed everything else into the background. I began to carve out a place in the school as a respected teacher. As I had found out in Ile-a-la-Crosse, I thrived most as a teacher when working with high school students. Within weeks, I found myself taking on the role of a coach for the school's cross-country running team, and boys' soccer team. Life had become packed with activity, both at home and at school.

At home things began to change. The lack of trust in me had caused a shift in our relationship. With that tension and silent distrust, I began to lose confidence in my role in the family. I retreated at times, to standing on the sidelines. The last thing I wanted to do was to make another wrong decision that would test our eight-year-old marriage. With a power vacuum created, Marynia stepped in to take control of the finances and our life as a family. I accepted the power shift with a measure of relief. With her taking the lead, there was less chance of me making another wrong choice.

We navigated the changing face of our relationship with its shifting of our roles. Marynia began to emerge as the dominant force in the family, while I took my energy into teaching and coaching, areas where I did best.

As the months passed, both began to settle into these new roles, and began to find our place within the community. With the passing months, our relationship improved. Time heals. With the familiar environment of rural and small-town life on the prairies, Marynia began to relax. Her previous anxiety that came with finding herself and her young family constantly on the move, was finally laid to rest. Our new home was soon filled with extended-family visitors and new friends. Being in the southern half of the province had made it much easier to feel connected.

Yet, somehow, it wasn't quite perfect. I had begun to disappear in tiny bits and pieces. It wasn't noticeable at first. I was unconsciously reverting to the strategies learned and practiced as a youth, focused on pleasing others. I found myself retreating to the sidelines. I was engaged enough to avoid appearing to be stuck up or rude, smiling frequently to cover up an emerging depression.

With the arrival of spring, I returned to running. I ran early in the morning before getting ready for school. While running, I felt confident and competent. Running also allowed me to silence the ghosts that had faintly begun to whisper in quiet moments. I had taken on the role of track coach, coaching by example, teaching what I knew as a runner. The doubts I had about myself began to fade with the adrenalin rush of running and coaching others. Running was one territory where I had total control.

Like magic, in that spring of 1980, a son we named Dorian, was born. I was surprised, not so much that I finally had a son, but that I was now a father to a son. I resolved not to treat him like my father had treated me. I was determined to become more present in the family, and within the community.

The next seven years passed in a rush with the routines of normal family and community life. My work was progressing well, and our family's standing in the community was ascending, as both of us had invested time and energy in the community. We participated in the community events, especially in activities in which our children were involved.

Both Marynia and I coached sports in which our children were taking part, when a coach was needed. Marynia focused on girls' softball and soccer, while I led a cross-country running club, became a hockey coach and manager, and helped with minor baseball. Together, we formed a small cross-country skiing club for our children and friends. There was no "me" time for either of us as our young, growing family became more and more active.

We went camping at every opportunity from late spring to mid-autumn. Sometimes we camped alone as a family, and at other times with other families. As the years passed, and as occasions allowed, we began to skinny dip as a family under the cover of darkness. It was an exhilarating and fun experience for all. Under the cover of darkness, there wasn't any shame in being nude. We hadn't skinny dipped since our stay in Ile-a-la-Crosse. Why it had reappeared, was a mystery.

In 1982, I had resumed university studies with the intention of getting a second university degree, a Bachelor of Arts degree. I intended in majoring in French. In 1984, I had become an executive member of the provincial French Teachers' Association. And in 1986, I had begun to participate in national pilot programs for the teaching French as a Second Language. It was the role where I could challenge myself. I needed challenges, professional challenges.

My teaching energy had begun to suffer from the repetitious covering of the same material using the same traditional methods of teaching a second language. I was bored with repetitive teaching strategies that were textbook and workbook based. Having finally caught up with the content I was teaching, I needed more challenges. As a result of my stretching outside of the classroom, my professional life blossomed.

"Marynia!" I called showing her a letter I held in his hand in the spring of 1987, "They are going to let me attend the workshop in Montréal." I had applied to take part in a two-week workshop for new second-language teaching methods.

Marynia was proud of my accomplishments as a teacher. However, this news meant that I would be away from home for two weeks. We had never really spent any time apart from each other since we had been married. The two-week workshop was set to take place during the summer.

"I knew they would choose you, Bob. I mean, how could they not choose you? You should go a few days early so that you can see your Dad," she continued. "Deborah says that he's not doing well. She's afraid that he won't be coming back home from the hospital."

"I don't know," I muttered, "It's not like he's ever even tried to connect with us, with me. I mean, we try each time we take the kids to Ottawa, but it seems he just doesn't care." We had been making the journey to Ottawa every two years. The need to ensure our children knew their extended family on my side of the family had me concede to make these visits.

"But you're not your dad, Bob. I think you need to make this effort now, rather than regret it later. You remember how glad you felt after seeing your French grandfather before he died. You were at peace knowing you had seen him before he died. It's better than waiting for your dad's funeral when it would be too late." She was right. I was at peace in 1984 after having visited my grandfather less than a week before he died.

When summer arrived, and it was time to leave, Marynia and the three children walked with me to the bus station. After giving the children my trademark bear hugs and kisses, I gathered Marynia in my arms and whispered, "I'll love you always, all ways, and forever." Then I boarded the bus taking a seat beside the window where I could see them waiting for me to wave good-bye. As they stood there watching and waving, I saw tears fall from Marynia's eyes. I knew this journey to the East wasn't going to be easy for either of us.

In Ottawa I spent some time with one of my sisters, as well as taking the time to attend a CFL football game with my father. He was in very poor health. He had become an in-patient at the veterans' hospital. He was very weak, and as a result he couldn't manage to stay for the whole game before he had to return to the hospital. I didn't have the heart to say anything to upset him. Though I had so many questions about the past, shadows that were lurking in dim recesses, I did my best to make my father smile, to leave him with a positive memory.

The past didn't seem to matter anymore now that I was confronted, face-to-face, with my father's mortality. I wanted to give him as much joy as possible that sunny afternoon at the stadium. I subconsciously knew it was going to be the last time I would see my father. There would be no more biannual family trips to Ottawa which would include a stop to visit with him, his wife and her two sons. When I left Ottawa by train for Montreal, I was already beginning to grieve for the loss of my father.

The workshop taught me quite a few new teaching strategies with which would improve classroom instruction. I would use them to make lessons more interactive with the students.

I was one of two teachers from Saskatchewan who would be piloting this new approach to second-language teaching.

While involved with the workshops, I didn't realise just how much Marynia was suffering from my absence. I had always been there beside her, regardless of what was going on between us, and now I wasn't there. I was far away, interacting with others, others who were professionals. Marynia's self-doubts were gnawing away, leaving her questioning her own worth. 'What if he meets a smart woman: someone who has the same interests; someone who is beautiful? What if he leaves me for her?' were thoughts that haunted her.

Each evening, I phoned home, needing to talk with Marynia. "What did you do today, Love?" I asked hoping to have her talk of her day and about the children.

"Nothing important. Just the usual, feed the kids and then wait for your phone call." Marynia couldn't bear to ask questions about my day, as that always opened a floodgate as I excitedly told her about what I had learned, and what I had hoped to try in the classroom when I returned. My enthusiasm stood in stark contrast to her feelings of abandonment, her certainty that she wasn't worthy of me, and that I would leave her once I found someone else.

I heard a different story in the prolonged silences during our phone calls. My own self-worth issues told me that she had finally realised just how much better off she was without me in the picture. It was no wonder that she had so little to tell me. As I held onto her prolonged silences, I began to panic within myself. And, I couldn't find the words to bridge the silence.

"I'm tired and need to go to bed, Bob. We'll talk tomorrow, okay?"

"Okay, Babe. Tomorrow. I love you, Marynia."

"Me too," she returned before again retreating into a silence.

The distance that had grown between me and Marynia while I was in Montreal during the summer of 1987, didn't fully disappear when I returned home. However, we both shrugged it off, as we again immersed ourselves into another school year and the raising of three children. Besides the usual activities, we had agreed to lead a trip to France for my senior French students during the following Easter break. Marynia had agreed to be the female chaperone for the trip, even knowing it would mean being away from the children for ten days. I had hoped that somehow the trip through France, Italy, and Switzerland would rekindle the magic in our marriage.

The time until the departure for France in April 1988, went by quickly. The work of trying to reformat teaching instruction to fit with the new methods of teaching a second language consumed most of my free time. Once the new school year was underway, I began having visitors come to the classroom to observe these new methods in action. My professional status grew stronger both inside and outside of the school as a result.

With the preparations for the France trip, as well as the ordinary everyday stuff of living in a small town on the Canadian prairies, I found it necessary to cut back on sleep time. In the background behind the scenes of this even busier life, I had begun to have nightmares, another reason for me to avoid sleep. Cracks were also beginning to appear beneath the surface. I was deferring more and more to Marynia's choices in daily decision-making. And with my pulling back even more from a shared responsibility to the family, Marynia's anger began to simmer. Both of us were increasingly on edge.

The trip to Europe went well. We guided twenty-five students through France, then Italy, and then into

Switzerland. Late one evening while in Nice, while the students were doing their own thing, Marynia and I went down to the Mediterranean Sea to walk along the shore, a rare moment without students around us. With the warmth of the evening air, and seeing a quiet and secluded corner, I decided to skinny-dip in the Mediterranean Sea. It was an impulsive choice. The water was cold, making the adventure a quick in and out experience. Once out of the water, I hurriedly put my clothing back on because of the cold. Skinny-dipping rekindled something in me that was reflected in my eyes. Seeing that spark and my grin, Marynia laughed. This was the Bob she remembered, as I stood before her with a mischievous grin on my face.

Back home in Canada, with the France trip completed and with other extra-curricular activities lessening in intensity, I began to again slip into a quiet depression. My father had died in May, not long after our return from France. I intuitively knew there was something wrong within me, but I didn't know what it was. I felt numb with the news of his death. I told Marynia that I didn't have to go to the funeral, that I didn't want to go. I wrote my depression off as natural grieving, even though I had no feelings whatsoever in relation to the news of his death. What I did feel was a hole left within myself that needed filling. Even getting a Bachelor of Arts degree with distinction in the spring of 1989 didn't lift my spirits.

Falling into another depression had left me without much desire, with less energy, and without a sense of purpose in my life. Being a husband and father didn't seem to be enough, especially when I believed that I had failed as both a husband and as a father.

Because of the depression, I never got around to planning a second trip to France for the spring of 1990. Depression had robbed me of the energy needed for planning. In another attempt to fill the hole with me, I had embarked on a new series of university classes for a planned Master of Educational Psychology degree. I truly believed I just needed to keep busy. The problem was that it didn't really take much energy to do the classes. I was consistently the oldest in my classes, and it didn't take a lot of effort to succeed. I did well in even though I wasn't giving the courses the attention they deserved.

Repressed libido, one's vital energy life force, needs to go somewhere. It wasn't going into my teaching which had become automatic, repeated scripts even with the changes in teaching style. It wasn't going into community activities, as I found myself withdrawing into a more passive presence within those activities. And, it wasn't going into my marriage, which had begun to suffer because of my lack of libido, my lack of energy.

The nightmares and night storms began to become more frequent. And when daylight finally came, neither of us talked about those night storms. We both retreated and braved the daytime hours as co-conspirators, united in facing the outer world. No one would ever know or guess that all wasn't well in our home.

Chapter Nine – Immersion Into Running and Psychology

I was always running away from something ... 1988.

Life in the small prairie town continued to unfold with an outward normality for Marynia and me. Our children were growing older. As a couple, we continued to lead active lives both in school and out of school. Marynia had become busy with a career in the emergency response field, as manager of the ambulance service, and with the teaching of First Aid and CPR. And with the change in my studies now focusing on psychology, my self-worth improved, and the depression receded. A sense of purpose and meaning returned. I had rediscovered the passion for psychology and philosophy. I had abandoned both when I left Nelson following my first year of university. One course focused on the various methods and schools of psychotherapy. Within that class, I experienced dream work. The professor had explained the role of dreams in working with counselling clients. Following his encouragement, I agreed to lead the class of young adults in a group session using a Gestalt approach to dream work.

Before the agreed upon time for the dream session, I broadened my research to see what else there was to be learned about working with dreams. I discovered the work of Carl Jung and his approach to dream work. I instantly knew I had struck a gold mine. With the research done, I led the group, including the professor as a participant, using a dream offered by one of the students. Feeling flushed with success following the class, I returned to the library and signed out a few books written by C.G. Jung. I then began to dream of becoming a Jungian analyst.

Back home, life improved. Plans were made for a second student trip to France. Both Marynia and I planned on having a trip every second year, as it would allow us to eventually take each of our three children to France. By the time the planning was done, with only nine students registered, I realised that I would be taking the students to France by myself. For a second chaperone, there had to be twelve students participating. I was ready to simply cancel the trip, but Marynia was adamant that the trip needed to happen. The school and the community would come to expect it when it was time for our children to take part in the France trips.

My outer life wasn't as under control as I had believed. I began to have interpersonal issues with a few people at school. Some dysfunction was again seeping out. I had no idea that the negative conflicts beginning to appear in my professional life, had roots in my past, roots that were arising in tortured dreams. It wasn't just in dreams, and in my professional life, but in my relationship with Marynia that conflict began to renew.

"I can't take this anymore, Bob!" protested Marynia following another night storm.

Hearing those words, yet again, I retreated from the centre of the bed to cling to the edges, almost to the point of falling off the bed. I retreated from Marynia's pain into silence, shame, and a tenseness that left me struggling to breathe.

"Talk to me! What's the matter with you?" Tears began to course down her cheeks as she wrapped herself in a hug.

I felt her pain, knowing that it was all my fault. I loved her and couldn't bear to see her in pain. And like all other times when she pulled into herself in some sort of grief, I moved towards the centre of the bed where she lay cocooned. Then, I wrapped my arms around her while murmuring almost wordless expressions of love.

"Dammit! Talk to me. It feels like you've left me, like you're getting ready to leave me alone with our three children."

"There's no one else, Marynia. Just you. I know that I'm not worth being loved by you. I don't blame you for wanting me out of the bed and out of our home. Life would be so much better for all of you if I just disappeared."

And that is how I felt. I had no place to run to, no person I wanted to escape to. I was becoming tired, physically and mentally tired. But, even more than that, I was beginning to give up. Nothing made sense anymore. I loved Marynia more than I loved living. I loved my children. Yet, as Marynia kept telling me, love wasn't enough. I had to be present, to be a real part of their life, wanting to be there and celebrating being there.

My mind reeled. '*I have it all,*' I thought. '*I have everything a man could ever ask for. I have a loving and beautiful wife. I*

*have three incredible children. I have a career and a
community that respects me. Why is this happening to me?'*
Yet, there I was, sinking into darkness and despair. And like
all others who sink into darkness, my first response was to
blame others for the depression. Those who held real
authority over me were the first to shoulder the blame.
Feeling the pressure that naturally came with less energy to
put into my work as a teacher, school authority became
resented. Rightly or wrongly, the school administration had
denied me the role of student counsellor though I had the
only training in educational psychology of all the school's
staff. All that mattered was that I believed it had been a
personal attack on me. Despite what I believed, the school
administration continued to support all the other projects that
I had undertaken, including the use of a computer in the
classroom, the only such project in the school division at that
time.

It wasn't just the obvious authority of the school
administration, I came to believe that even with my
involvement in coaching, I was being unfairly treated and
diminished by others after so many years as coach and
manager of various teams. Depression kept me from realising
that the others who had taken on roles I had once held, had
done so because they had a stronger background and
understanding of the team sports, and more importantly,
because I had become less present in those roles. It didn't
help that I began to make mistakes due to my divided
attention between increased responsibilities as a teacher and
as a university student.

However, it was the blaming of Marynia for having stopped
loving me that did the most damage to my self-worth. I had
abdicated control, bit by bit over the years while living in
Lanigan. What I gave up in control, created a vacuum which
Marynia had to step into so that the family would not suffer.
It fell to Marynia to make more and more of the decisions

about family life and community life. It wasn't that I didn't want to make decisions, rather I didn't have the needed energy or confidence in myself to negotiate a shared path through decision-making. As Marynia came to take on a stronger role in charting the way forward, I saw her as usurping my role, leaving me feeling even less of a man. And because of a growing insecurity, an unconscious anger began to swell deep within, an anger that I swallowed leaving me resentful and increasingly even more ill-at-ease with myself.

The trigger had been my father's death. His death had not allowed me time or opportunity to address painful questions about my childhood with him. our last time together was spent on keeping things calm, with me not daring to ask questions. I unconsciously resentment my father for this final loss, and it infected all my relationships with those who had some authority in my life. I was regressing from a mature, adult male into a brooding shadow of a man.

The world around me became negatively charged, became a dark swampland that appeared ready to swallow me. People around me took on extra-human attitudes, almost as if they were dark entities that sought to devour me. Marynia, who had carried the heavy burden of being my Magical Other, had now, somehow morphed into the Dark Queen. Fear became my response to this darker universe.

Why was this happening to me? Was it just because my father had died, a man who had abused his authority as a father? The answer was 'yes and maybe'. Yes, his death served to awaken something in me that had been hidden, denied, and then eventually forgotten for the most part since I had become a man. Maybe, because there were things in my current life, in which men with authority were unconsciously complicit, dealing with their own issues of power and authority. These were only some of the questions that went unasked and unanswered. I had entered an in-between world where a man had to reconcile the first half of life with the present life, so as to move consciously into the future. I had begun to suffer a midlife crisis.

Loss of soul. The loss of libido, the loss of one's life force and energy, is characteristic of a midlife crisis. Most forms of psychology and psychotherapy have no room for soul, and as a result have no strategies for dealing with a midlife crisis other than through medication. Psychology distances itself from the very idea of soul in its attempt to appear as a legitimate science-based approach to mental health. The word soul is too wrapped up in religious dogma. My studies of psychology led me into a place in which I had once wandered as a youth, the world of depth psychology and philosophy. In those areas, the ancient idea of soul was still alive and well.

It is hard to believe in the existence of something, anything, until that something disappears and leaves one with a sense of loss. We feel the loss as a feeling of emptiness. This is probably the truest for soul. For most people, the soul is a religious concept that one accepts without question or rejects. Anyone who is not a "believer" generally accepts that the scientific belief that the soul is simply a delusion, a figment created by religions to have people ignore the bad things happening to them and to those around them. Yet, there comes a point when some people search for answers that resonate with more than just what the head, what the ego tells them. Perhaps, it has to do with the fact that the word soul has become too broad and as such, almost meaningless in the process.

I, like so many others, felt my world beginning to fall apart. Yet, when looked at from the outer world, everything seemed to be going on as it had always gone on. The outer world was oblivious of the panic and fear that raged within me. I didn't know it at that time, but I had been given the "call" to take back ownership of my life. My life path had reached a crossroads. Which way would I turn? Would I follow the call to embark on a hero's journey through the darkness, or turn and run?

I had studied enough psychology to begin to recognise what was happening to me. To be honest, most of the time the simple process of teaching, studying, and being a parent allowed me to be fully present without the pressure of the past or the present triggering my complexes. I believed that if I could only wait it out until the children had finished their schooling, I would willingly follow the call. And so, I scrambled for escape routes in order to avoid dealing with the approaching darkness within me, especially when one or more of my complexes were activated.

I didn't want any more pain. I had worked hard to escape the poverty I had lived within while growing up. I worked hard to have a family and had become a respected member of a community. What else was I supposed to do? My Magical Other had become a fallible human, no longer a goddess on a pedestal. That was an unbearable loss. There was nothing inside of me left to hold onto. However unknown to me, Marynia was suffering her own pain and had very little energy or will left to be the caretaker of my soul.

The man she had married had effectively disappeared. I was now a man who cowered in dark corners, unsure of myself, and unable to make decisions. Yet, Marynia held on to me as much as she held on to herself. Both of us held on tightly to our marriage as if it was our life raft, unwilling to admit defeat. The central focus for both of us were the children. The extended family, engagement to the community, and our careers were our life jackets.

Chapter Ten – Computer-Mediated Communication vs Reality

When I tore myself away from pain into family, there was real joy.
The trip to France for 1991 went well. The smaller group of nine students tested me only to find that I was still a man who abided by the rules set for the group by the school and parents. Despite my tendency to be rigid, the trip had more than enough positive experiences for the students. Almost as soon as we had returned home, the younger students began to plead for their turn. I realised that I had done this. I had pulled it off on my own without having to depend on someone else to make all the last minute and day-to-day decisions that came with guiding teenagers through three European countries.

With our first daughter, Nola, being a part of the group planning on going to France for 1993, we worked consciously, together to create a good experience for that next France trip. Marynia's commitment to be the female chaperon took a lot of stress off the planning for me. Less than a month after the return to the school in the late spring of 1991, enough students and their parents had committed to the next France trip, ensuring Marynia's participation in the planning, the fundraising, and as chaperone.

At the school, there was some reaction by a few female teachers, reaction as to why I would choose Marynia for the role of chaperone, rather than a female teacher since it was a school event. The parents trusted Marynia and wanted her to take on the role of chaperone which was the deciding factor.

I continued with my studies in psychology at the university. Filling in the hours with teaching, coaching, running and taking classes at the university was enough to keep the darkness contained. The next year passed without serious emotional issues for me. Life had finally returned to a somewhat normal state. With a united focus on things other than our relationship, Marynia and I somehow dodged the blows that could have destroyed our marriage. Life was as good as it could be given the darkness that bubbled uneasily beneath the surface.

In the early summer of 1992, I entered a Master of Education program with the focus on Instructional Technology. Though I had originally planned on registering for the Educational Psychology program, a new Master of Education program had caught my attention. I soon found myself caught up in the idea that I could become a world leader in the field of distance education using computer technology. This was something I knew would put me firmly into the good books of the school administration, and at the same time, appeal to my students.

The decision to abandon the psychology degree wasn't based on logic. I was distracted by novelty, the magical world of cyberspace. My psyche wasn't ready to be immersed into the world of psychology. My ego was still too fragile. With a new focus, and now with an Internet account which I could access from home using a modem, I entered the new world of Computer-Mediated Communication. And with that decision made, I felt a surge of energy, a return of libido into my life. Unknowingly, I had made the right choice. I began to connect with people who challenged the world as it was. There were no judgments by others based on normal outer-world status indicators; all accepted each other through their online presence created by the words that appeared on a computer screen. Judgment was reserved for what one said, the ideas that emerged in computer-mediated dialogue. I believed I became more visible through my words, and more respected for ideas I could never speak within the confines of my face-to-face world. My confidence grew as I mingled with others who had doctorates, others who were authors, and others who had the respect of so many in their personal, face-to-face worlds. With them, I had become an equal. It was intoxicating, and it gave me a psychological high.

Unknown to me and the others engaging on the Internet, there was a danger with an immersion into the world of cyberspace, the danger of becoming even more disconnected in the daily outer-world life. With more energy invested in being present in cyberspace communications, there was less energy for being present in one's everyday life. I didn't know about Internet addiction as the term didn't exist yet. Few people had any access to the Internet in the days before the World Wide Web. I rationalised my constant connection to this inner world, seeing it as necessary to meet my new educational goals. Regardless of that rationale, I became addicted to engaging with spirit in cyberspace. My soul had found a different place in which to be projected.

Despite the unknown dangers of Internet addiction, I did discover treasure in the experiments with Computer-Mediated Communication [CMC]. I brought the modem to school, then connected it to a school computer using a very long telephone line which was strung to my classroom. My students soon became engaged in experimental, text dialogues with other second-language students in other parts of the world. The conversations with others had begun to build a network upon which I drew, enhancing the classroom experiences for the students. Though most in the community didn't understand much about the computer or about the Internet, I was viewed as a wise person, an explorer of sorts who brought back treasure for my students and community.

The next two years passed with only a few night storms between Marynia and me. We had immersed ourselves in our respective areas of interest and careers. If anyone would have looked in from the outside, they would have believed that we had it all. Did we believe it? It was a question neither of us asked, though we both knew that there was trouble brewing beneath the surface. The France trip of 1993 went off without any negative results. And as soon as those students returned, the next group of students were clamouring to begin their turn at planning sessions.

By 1994, I had shifted focus from CMC and second-language teaching, to exploring the possibility of using CMC for psychotherapy and counselling in cyberspace. It seemed to be the perfect environment for psychology and making a difference in the world. I was drawn into this alter-universe as I pushed to explore ideas in depth. Somewhere along the way, I began to write poetry. And then, there were responses and resonances to my words cast adrift in cyberspace.

Without realising what had been taking place, the portal to the personal and collective unconscious had been opened like some Pandora's Box. What appeared in the poetry and in the dialogues in cyberspace, were the voices of my soul projected upon others who heard echoes of their own soul. I had cast my soul into the ether of cyberspace, casting a handful of tiny hooks into that limitless ocean, with no real intention or expectation of catching anything. The projections were cast out, and there were others in cyberspace who heard the voice behind the poems, others who believed they had found their missing soulmate, their Magical Other, reflected in those words I had written.

With every resonance heard in the responses of others, my self-esteem blossomed. I began to think that I would find myself as a pure soul, a Buddha-like being, a wise saint-like presence somewhere in cyberspace. In the world of cyberspace, projection flies freely, especially when all that is used to communicate are the words spoken and heard. We each create our unique and personal version of the voices heard. Each person in the CMC dialogues creates an image of the Other who was responding to their words. There were no scars, no imperfections that marked these Others.

I sensed, at least on a subconscious level, that I was somehow cheating on Marynia, not in a physical sense, but at a much deeper level. What had held the marriage together through all the years, had been a unified commitment to children, as well as a deep-rooted stubbornness that didn't allow us to take the easy way out. My immersion into cyberspace was testing both of us. We both retreated into a silent truce while wearing forced smiles in public and in front of our children. We rarely admitted the truth to each other, even in the middle of night storms, that something was poisoning our marriage. We fought about the surface conditions of life, quiet fights so that the children would not hear us in the middle of the night.

Another trip to France took place during the 1995 Easter break. The trip in 1993, had gone well with Nola. It was the perfect way to end her high school studies before heading off to college. Our second daughter, Natalie, and her classmates were excited to go on their own France trip after watching the slide show, and the video of her sister's trip.

The time between these two trips was all about maintaining life as normal as possible. We were aware that regardless of how most of our life together appeared to be an amazing and happy story, beneath the surface I was suffering from something that had nothing to do with our present life together. It was a suffering that began to manifest itself physically. Whatever was roiling below the surface had found its way into severe back and hip pain. I had quit running because of heel spurs which meant the loss of even that small passion. I found myself struggling more than usual when we returned from the 1995 trip. Because of the growing unrest in our marriage, and my addiction to the Internet, I struggled in holding myself together, trying harder and harder to hold onto sanity.

The female teacher who had once been considered as a France trip replacement for Marynia, began to appear in my dreams. Those dreams ridiculed me as a man, taunted me as being an impotent man. Marynia heard me speak her name in my sleep. '*What was going on? Is he having an affair? Is he going to leave me and the children for her?*' were thoughts that tortured her as much as the dreams tortured me. Whatever trust was left between us, was weakening even more.

Chapter Eleven – Suicidal Thoughts and Depression

A birthday and a forced smile, 1994.

Feeling increasingly suicidal as 1995 began to unfold, I realised that I desperately needed help. In a state of panic which was shared by Marynia, I reached out to the Saskatchewan Teachers' Federation counselling services. I had hoped that in making this effort to engage in counselling as a client rather than as a counsellor, my life would change for the better, that counselling would in some way, fix me.

I began counselling with a man who looked more like a lumberjack than a mental-health professional, in the late spring of 1995. Over the remainder of the school year, counselling allowed me to calm down enough to successfully navigate the hurdles at work as a teacher. However, I still continued to think about suicide, something I had not done since my teenage years in Ottawa. With my counsellor,

Marvin's help, I made it through the rest of the school year. I then hoped that a summer break would make all the difference in my being more balanced for the following school year.

Yet, the world of cyberspace claimed more and more of my energy and attention. I became more and more sensitive to the slightest hints of criticism from the people around me at work and in the community. I retreated into the computer room with curtains drawn, hiding from the light at every possible opportunity.

Marynia feared for my life as I fell, deeper and deeper, into depression and irrational behaviours. I had begun to beat myself with my fists flying into my face. I raged at the slightest criticism. My anger was typically punctuated punches to my head. I didn't trust myself not to physically lash out at Marynia or the children. Marynia learned to tread carefully around me fearing that I would go too far in one of my rages. She began to fear me, the man who had been so gentle in the past. And then I began to spill out the secrets of my childhood, memories long forgotten began to surface. She learned that whatever it was that was driving me mad, it wasn't her or the children. It went much deeper.

Summer turned into fall only to find that I was almost incapable of managing a day of teaching. The only part of the day that seemed to give me some relief was the engagement of my French classes with other French-as-a-second-language classes through the Internet. In the world of Computer-Mediated Communication, I was the expert, the undisputed authority. I continued the master's program throughout the turmoil raging within me.

Just as the cross-country running season was winding down in the fall of 1995, I realised that if I didn't do something drastic to resolve my worsening mental health, I wouldn't survive much longer. The darkness had become too overwhelming. Marvin, shocked at the nose dive in my mental state, rushed to have me included in a psychotherapy retreat with other teachers who had found themselves unable to continue teaching. The retreat was to begin on the last day of the running season. With the school administration's permission, I arranged to have another teacher take the students home from the cross-country competition following the awards ceremony. I would then drive to the retreat site directly from the competition site before the presentation of awards.

I drove as fast as I could to the retreat site on the shores of Lake Diefenbaker, often hitting speeds in excess of 150 kilometres per hour on the rough country roads. As I drove, I dwelled on thoughts of veering off the road to intentionally crash into a telephone pole, or to swerve into the path of an oncoming large farm truck. Perhaps it was cowardice, though I told myself it was because of the pain and shame that suicide would inflict on my children and Marynia, that kept me on the road. Still, I drove on, pushing as fast as I could, to reach the retreat centre.

There was no need to rush, to drive like a madman. That first evening was simply a time for registration. Only a few of the retreat staff had arrived by the time I arrived at the site. After settling into my room, I took out my journal, a new book purchased just days before, along with a set of new felt, coloured pens. I began to tell myself in writing, why I was there and not back at home where I belonged. Somehow, writing became a religious experience. I wrote with great care. The choice of words mattered, and the penmanship mattered. With the first words recorded in the journal, I left the room. I slipped out of the building to wander through the trees along the edge of the lake, in the late afternoon. I wasn't ready to meet others who were now arriving and settling into their own small rooms.

Later that evening, we met for the first time and were given the rules for the weeklong retreat: no caffeine, and no romantic or sexual liaisons between the participants. We were then introduced to the leaders of the retreat, which included my counsellor, Marvin. When the group was dismissed, I went outside to be alone rather than mingle with the others. I wasn't here to be social. I was here because I was broken and needed fixing.

The next morning, one of the counsellors went through the process of teaching us meditation as part of the healing process. The work of the retreat was to teach the skills that would help us on our private journeys of healing, skills that we could continued to use once the retreat had ended. The group meditated as a group, three times each day. Soft music played in the background as we were guided to places of safety in our minds. Structured group therapy sessions followed, therapy sessions that were intent on teaching behavioural strategies for navigating safely through the darker moments.

One of the activities had participants take turns standing alone within a circle and then placing others within the circle representing those closest to the centre from within the group. When it was my turn, I had all the others in the group crowd into the centre of my circle. Then I left the circle to stand outside the group. For some reason, as I placed each person within the circle, they felt good about being included within the inner circle. But that changed to shock when I left the circle. I had created dissonance within the group. I had settled for total honesty without consciously realising that in doing so, I had evoked distress in the others. I didn't believe I had any worth in comparison with the others who were at the retreat. I didn't recognise that the others were also struggling.

When in group sessions and at mealtimes, I was a pleasant and considerate person. If anyone had been observing, there would have been little indication that I was a client in counselling and therapy sessions. If anything, I could easily have been taken to be one of the counsellors at the retreat. I tried everything that was asked of me. However, my responses were constrained and passive. I was a person encased in medieval armour and nothing was going to pierce that protective barrier.

I cried a lot during the retreat. I didn't cry during the session in front of others. That would have disclosed too much. Late at night, I would find a quiet corner, away from others. There, huddled in the darkness and holding my knees to my chest, I would cry silently. When I was finally exhausted, I would retreat into my private room and write in the journal before finally falling into a fitful sleep, filled with strange dreams.

When the retreat ended, I had somehow released most of the pent-up tensions that had marked my life before the retreat. Despite my passive resistances, something inside shifted. I was able to return home and go back to work, a more functional person. Helpful strategies learned, allowed me to maintain the gains made at the retreat. I returned to practicing meditation, something that I had abandoned once I had begun teaching. For the first time since I could remember, I felt hopeful. I began to pull myself back together. The retreat had done its work.

Yet, with the return home, I learned that I had left a trail of broken hopes and fears at home and in the community. The ripples that followed in the wake of my needing to go to the retreat had affected my family, as well as others who knew me as a friend and colleague. My mental breakdown had shocked them, leaving them unsure of just how to deal with me. I was able to navigate through the rest of the first semester, then Christmas and the New Year without another crisis. And, as a result, life dared to return to a hesitant new normal.

I had begun to hope again. The worst part of the haunting darkness that had plagued me, retreated into inner depths. Believing I was only going to get better and stronger going forward, I was able to smile and meet the world again. The worst was now safely behind me. And, at the beginning of 1996, our eldest child, Nola got married. Life was good and was getting better.

-

In early 1996, as with every other school year, it was time for a teachers' convention. Conventions were a diversion for the most part with teachers getting more out of being released from teaching for two days, than from the content of the seminars and presentations which were attended. However, in 1996 it was different for me. I attended a session led by Kelly Walker called "Soul Loss", a session that examined what happened when a person suffered burnout. I was surprised at what I heard:

> *"Midlife is a time for new awakenings. Crisis. Yes. Awakening to the TRUTH often causes us to abandon hitherto valid life scripts in honour of new truth. What a pity that this often causes deep wounds in those around us. Perhaps that is why we ought to go to the desert for period of time. Alone."*

Midlife. I found something in that word that felt like a lifejacket. I continued to listen to Kelly Walker while sitting on the edge of my chair, knowing that what I was hearing was vital to my well-being and journey. I now had a name for what had happened to me during the past few years.

> *"It is soul loss that happens when the good, generous and often very successful, in most aspects of life, women and men begin to fall apart from the inside out. Generally, it is the outer shell that is the last to break down. The inner breakdown has been going on for some time before it appears."*

I wrote furiously as the presentation went on. Almost everything Walker talked about described what had been happening to me. I had been suffering soul loss, a midlife crisis. As soon as the session ended, I met some of the other staff members and recommended the session to them. A few were curious and followed up on the suggestion.

I left the conference more energized than I had felt for years. I rushed home to tell Marynia about what Kelly Walker had said in the presentation, holding the booklet I had purchased. My enthusiasm was infectious and Marynia began to believe. By holding on to me through the breakdown, the Bob she married, returned. With the intention to study more and find more answers about the issue of midlife crisis, I went on the hunt for as much information as I could find.

I found a book called, The Survival Papers: Anatomy of a Midlife Crisis, by Daryl Sharp, a Jungian analyst. An interesting fact about Daryl Sharp was that he had spent part of his childhood in Lanigan. That book led me to other books by other Jungian analysts. I was flying high as if in a manic state, certain that these books held all the answers I needed. With knowledge I would be freed from the depression that was intent on devouring me. As a bonus, in my mind, was the idea that what I learned could then be used to help others.

That high began to fade. Knowledge wasn't the real issue. In the rush to understand, the words quoted by Daryl Sharp in the introduction to his first chapter: *"When an inner situation is not made conscious, it happens outside as fate,"* hadn't registered. There was too much I didn't know about myself, stuff hidden and denied from the past. And until that stuff was dealt with, I would continue to sway between manic highs and depressed lows, suffering as a victim of the past, blaming fate and blaming others.

Despite the discovery of books by Daryl Sharp and James Hollis, and the convention presentation by Kelly Walker, I had work to do in life. I had a final half class to complete the requirements for the master's program. Digging deeper into Jungian psychology would have to wait. Regardless of my efforts to focus on that last half class, another project involving a chapter for a book called K to 12 Online, and my resolution to get my act together as a teacher, I continued to invest too much time and energy in cyberspace. I spread myself thin with multi-tasking so that there was little hope of anything getting done well.

I brought together all I had learned from classroom experiments with on-line communication, and my engagement with various on-line discussion groups, to craft a thesis proposal. I presented the proposal to the chair of my thesis committee. The plan was rejected as presented. The chairperson didn't want me to write a thesis, but to take a project route. Rather than a qualitative thesis approach, I was told to write up quantitative, statistic-backed study.

I left the meeting shaken and discouraged. I knew that I needed this man's approval if the thesis was to ever be accepted. There was no way I wanted to do a project instead of a thesis. I needed to write a meaningful document that would make a difference to the teaching of second languages using computer-mediated communication.

I did consider re-approaching the thesis with some of the objective data needed for project route proposed by the chairman. I went back to my classes in Lanigan with a series of questionnaires for the students to complete. The data from the questionnaires would become the statistical component of the thesis. I wondered how I could possibly blend those statistics into the qualitative approach of a thesis. An anger began to grow within me as I struggled with this necessity. Surprisingly, that anger was the fuel that allowed me to complete the school year without incident at home or school. The thesis, and my advisor, became the new enemy.

93

During the late spring of 1996, I had been asked to be one of the coaches for the zone track and field competitions. Those competitions would qualify athletes for competition in the following summer's Jeux de Canada Games to be held in Brandon, Manitoba. I persuaded a few of the school's athletes to take part in the event. All those who had placed well in the school district competition and at provincial completion were automatically given invitations to the Zone competitions.

I added three other athletes to the team to represent the zone in the race walk and hammer throw events as these weren't included in the High School Provincial Championships. The top two finishers in each event at these provincial, zone games would go on to compete at the national games the following summer.

Both race-walk competitors qualified for nationals, the female athlete winning her event and the male athlete who was my son, Dorian, getting the silver medal. I finished the school year with a firm belief that the future was now turning out for the better. I was going to finish the master's degree, my son was going to compete at Nationals, my reputation as a track coach, was spreading, and I was seen and recognised as an expert in the world of computers and the Internet. And, perhaps most important, we were going to celebrate our twenty-fifth wedding anniversary at the end of the summer.

-

Once the school year was done, I was given an office to use for the summer at the university. I could work uninterrupted whenever I made the trip to the city. It wasn't long before I took a sleeping bag to the office so that I could spend a few nights there saving gas money. It gave me enough alone time to finish the thesis. Before submitting the thesis, I had several other professors, who were long-time acquaintances, read it.

These other professors assured me that I had written a solid and defensible thesis.

However, the chairperson still wasn't satisfied. He again suggested that the thesis be scrapped, and that I should write it up as a project, with a greater focus on producing even more statistical evidence over a longer period of time. He told me to bring the project back to him the following year. I returned home discouraged.

I knew I couldn't go back to work on the thesis anymore. I missed too much of my life at home and in the community. The thesis had become all about my ego, not about fulfilling myself, or healing myself. When I told the Dean of Education of my intentions to settle for Post Graduate Diploma, he tried to talk me out of abandoning the thesis. He had read the thesis and knew that it was almost ready for publication. He suggested that I reconsider and proposed assigning a new chairperson for the committee, a man who had been one of the men who had told me that what I had written was worthy of a thesis. I refused. I returned home feeling defeated and ashamed at having failed. I knew Marynia was there and that she still loved me and still wanted me in her life, and that was all that mattered.

And then, in that summer of 1996, I became a grandfather for the first time, the day before my forty-seventh birthday. I made a vow to do what I could to honour the role grandfather with this new member within the family.

Chapter Twelve – A Son's Accident and A Brother's Suicide

Feeling the pain of everything 1996.

The week before classes were to start in August 1996, Marynia phoned me while I was at school getting ready for another school year. She called to ask if I could help her at an accident scene. For the past few years, I had been a volunteer ambulance driver and attendant for the ambulance service that Marynia managed. Our son, Dorian, was one of three injured in a car rollover, his car. I shifted into Emergency Response mode as I rushed out of the school to help at the accident site. It took two ambulances to get the three teenagers to the hospital in Saskatoon. It wasn't until the last ambulance drove away with Marynia monitoring Dorian, when I found myself shaken to the core.

Dorian was in serious jeopardy. He had been the driver and was the most seriously injured. The car was totalled. I saw the damaged car and irrationally blamed myself. '*If only I had been home that summer, he wouldn't have been* . . .' I couldn't go home. I instinctively knew I couldn't be there alone. So, I returned to the school and buried myself in busy work. I didn't want to be alone as I would only think too much. I shuffled back from the book-storage room to the classroom with books for students, a task that didn't demand much focus. Later, when I was in the copy room preparing documents for opening week, various teachers stopped to ask how I was doing and if I had heard any news from Marynia. Everyone was very supportive. I needed them, these teachers whom I had almost abandoned. The realisation that these people were important to me, gave me something to lean on at that moment. Hearing their words, I was pulled back from a very dark place.

A few days later, we celebrated our twenty-fifth anniversary with these same people, our friends at the school. We had another reason to celebrate, a more important reason. Dorian was going to be okay.

Over the next several months, life again returned to some sort of quiet normalcy. There were no university classes to claim my time, so I focused more on strengthening my counselling skills. I worked to include more Gestalt strategies, as well as adding in Solution-Focused Therapy techniques following a provincial training workshop. I had increased my presence in the provincial association for counselling by becoming a member-at-large on the executive committee. As well, I returned to reading as many books as I could about Jungian psychology. Once again, I had begun to think about becoming a Jungian analyst when my teaching career was over, perhaps even sooner.

I had begun writing poetry again, something I hadn't done in almost twenty years. I wrote poetry in both English and French. The poetry betrayed the desperation of my self-imposed isolation. It betrayed how I had lost all respect for myself and felt abandoned. Within me, the distance between myself and the rest of the world grew. The poetry written told the story of a man in search of Eros, a search that projected Eros onto others both in day-to-day life and in cyberspace. Just before Christmas, I put the poems into a booklet, which I then gave to Marynia as a gift. I then gave copies to the staff at the school and was surprised at the positive response.

Then, in early 1997, one of my younger brothers committed suicide. Hearing the news, I buried myself in my home office and cried for both my brother and for myself. I sang "Go Rest High on That Mountain," to my brother. For the next few weeks I went through the days on autopilot, numb. I was sinking into depression again, and I knew I desperately needed to return to counselling. However, there was still Dorian's trip to France to take place at Easter time, only months away, and then Dorian's competition at the National Games in the summer. These two commitments served as significant anchors for me in the outer world. To occupy my mind, I began a series of at-distance courses for counselling certification.

The trip to France during the Easter break of 1997 with Dorian, and his classmates was an excellent experience for both Marynia and me, as well as the students. We both knew it was likely going to be the last such trip unless I could somehow escape my ongoing cyclical bouts of severe depression.

With the France trip done, the end of the school year in June 1997 became a descent into chaos. I had been unable to focus enough to keep individual records of my students' success and found it necessary to invent marks for them. I gave old exams to the students to help prepare them for the final exams, hoping that somehow the material being tested in these old exams had been taught. The results gave me data and proof that the course had been taught well enough for their success. When it was time for final exams, I photocopied old exams just hours before the exam was given. Surprisingly, no one seemed to have noticed. The students were satisfied with their marks. The school administration was satisfied as well.

It was only in my roles of father and coach that kept me from totally falling apart and giving in to the darkness.

Father

He is father, this stranger who walks bent under
unknown weights shouldering unknown sufferings.
A man's eyes tell of his separateness, his aloneness.
His remoteness leaves me feeling lost, feeling less.

He is father, this man who sits quietly at the table
who sits listening to the voices of family.
A man's silences tell of his journeys to fearful places
speak of his doubts, his sufferings, his needs.
His silence leaves me feeling abandoned, alone.

He is father, this man.

I spent a good part of the summer of 1997 with Dorian, training him as a race walker. Dorian was getting very good, and so I pushed him to be even better. At the Jeux de Canada Games, he finished fifth, with a personal best time for the ten-kilometre race. Dorian was the youngest athlete in the competition. His strong showing in the race had been noticed, and he was asked to take part in the Junior Pan-American Games. Dorian refused. Race walking was my passion, not his, and he knew it. Unknowingly, Dorian had taught me a vital lesson in standing up for himself, one that I would have to duplicate not many months later.

With a new school year ahead, Dorian's final year in high school, Marynia and I took an exchange student, a Mexican student into our home so that Dorian would have a new friend, a brother of sorts. It was Dorian's last year of high school and we wanted it to be his best year.

I began the 1997-1998 school year with renewed high expectations, vowing to be more professional in my work with year plans, semester plans, and course plans to guide my work. I endeavoured to return to keeping the teacher's daily journal up to date, and to ensure that it had good and reliable data for evaluation purposes. My ability to hold to those vows crumbled before the arrival of winter.

With the end of the cross-country season came another descent into depression, and having me call my counsellor, looking for more counselling sessions at a more frequent rate. My efforts at school beginning to fail. I needed to have more help than my counsellor could give me. Marvin encouraged me to find an analyst who would be able to dig deeper.

So began the search for a Jungian analyst. However, the closest analysts were living and working in Calgary, a seven-hour drive from Lanigan. I gathered the information needed for analysis with the thought that with the end of the school year in June, I could begin psychoanalysis with one of those Jungian analysts. All that was needed for me to somehow survive until the end of the school year. Then, with two full months of analysis, the depression would be alleviated enough so I could become a more functional teacher and husband when the 1998-1999 school year began.

My best efforts to regain mental control were failing badly. I found myself again huddled in the darkness, lost in tears and lost to fear. The night storms between Marynia and me had again resumed and had increased in frequency and intensity, leaving both of us shattered and afraid. I caught myself behaving erratically in both the school and the community. I wandered down back lanes at nights wanting to avoid the street lights. I needed the darkness where I could hide. I became obsessed with imagined terrors and dark, immoral longings.

The night before the last day of classes before the Christmas break, a night storm left me with bruised cheeks and black eyes. I had punched myself repeatedly. I only stopped lashing out when I was finally exhausted. I was in deeper trouble than I had ever been before. I knew I wouldn't be able to finish out the school year. It would be lucky if I could even finish the semester. I hid the bruises behind sunglasses that last day at school. I was thankful I would have two weeks to recover, for the bruises to heal, and allow me to regather enough strength to finish off the school year.

On Christmas morning, while the house was silent, as the first light appeared in the back yard, I was in my home office feeling as far from festive as one could possibly feel. Looking out the window into the back yard, I found words to capture the feeling, a poem written at that time only in French:

Matin silent, matin de Noël – A Silent Christmas Morning

Pas de bruit ce matin / It is silent this morning
Sauf pour un vent leger / Except for a soft breeze
Qui fait danser ... / That stirs
Sauf pour une horloge / Except for a clock
Qui fait voler ... / Marking the fleeing of time

Regarde par la fenêtre / Look through the window
Pas de neige / No snow greets the eyes
Seulement la terre endormie / Only the earth sleeping
Pas d'enfants / No children
Seulement la balançoire démunie / Only the swing swaying

Regarde dans le salon / Look into the living room

Un arbre garni de lumière / A tree decorated with lights
Un symbole visuel / Stands as a symbol
Un espoir promis et mystère / Of hope and promise
Ce matin de Noël / This Christmas morning

Somehow, I still had hope despite an overwhelming sense of loneliness. Our last child was still at home and he had turned into a young man. Too soon, even Dorian would be gone. Then I would have no excuses to avoid dealing with my issues. I would then be forced to confront myself and face what was happening to our marriage. The showdown was approaching. It would be coming sooner than I wanted or could have predicted.

Chapter Thirteen – Calgary and Jungian Psychoanalysis

The source of life and a totem
gifts of therapy and analysis, Calgary 1998.

It wasn't long after classes began following the Christmas break when I found myself again desperately panicking with the approaching semester exams and the need to find marks for the students. Marynia was alarmed with what she saw as I scrambled with last minute tests, again using copies of previous final exams to fill in the void. She asked our family doctor to meet with me. Tom, our family doctor, wasted no time in advocating for me to seek immediate mental-health help. Another appointment was made with Marvin.

I drove off to the city for an evening appointment in the second week back in classes, a week before semester final exams. Marvin was surprised to see how much I had regressed since our last session together. He listened as I talked and cried throughout the hour session. At the end of our session, Marvin gave me a task, I was to begin writing my life story. There was something hidden in the past that needed exposing, something that was pressing into my life and causing these downward spirals. And, he gave me a small stone, a totem, which I was to carry with me during the journey of healing.

Since journaling was a task that I had given to some of my own clients, I was familiar with what was expected and why this was so important. *'Why haven't I already done this?'* I wondered as I drove back to Lanigan. I was told to bring the journal for the next session set for a week later.

For the first time in my life, I deliberately sat down to confront the past, my past. I was done running from it, at least that is what I tried to tell myself. Whatever ghosts from the past were active, I was going to face them head on, listen to them. And so, I wrote.

Over the next few days, the words poured out. I wrote at home, and I wrote in my classroom while the students worked through past exams in preparation for their final exams. I even had the students mark each other's exams before recording the results. Finally, I would have some real data to use for report cards

When it was time to return to Marvin's office, I had thirty-seven pages of remembered history ready to give to him, pages I had shared with Marynia. Reading them, she began to realise that most of our troubles together had nothing to do with her, but with my past which had never been disclosed. As she had watched me over the week, she saw that the Bob she married was still there. That glimpse of the man she married was enough for her. She would be there for me throughout whatever was yet to come.

The session with Marvin focused on some of those remembered abuses. I talked about the physical abuse at the hands of my father, and about the chaotic changing of schools and addresses across different provinces. There were hints in the pages suggesting there was much more yet to be remembered. Yet, for the moment, it was all that I remembered. The counsellor again remarked at the end of the session that I needed to work with someone who could work at depth. The pressure within me eased and I was able to complete the semester without any further mishaps. I began to hope, again that I could make it to the end of the school year.

-

As the February break approached, I began to panic. Bits and pieces of the past were still emerging from the shadows where they had been hidden. I couldn't face going back to school with the sewage of the past pouring out and torturing me. A remembered incident of being sexually molested by my English grandfather shocked me the most. With that remembrance, a Pandora's Box of other sexual abuses by other adults began to surface. It wasn't just about physical and emotional abuses, or dissociation anymore. My dreams became charged with absurd sexual energy, with me as a helpless witness rather than as a participant. I went again to see our doctor to see if he knew a psychologist that could perhaps help me, as I couldn't wait for summer and access to a Jungian analyst.

The doctor sent me to see a psychiatrist he had heard of in the city. The psychiatrist responded with anger when I told her about the problems. She scolded me and told me to go back to work and stop looking for an excuse to get paid medical leave. I was stunned and frantic. A quick call to Marvin resulted in an emergency session with him. Between the counsellor, the doctor, and Marynia, it was decided that I couldn't delay with beginning intense psychotherapy in

Calgary. Calls were made to Calgary and interview appointments were arranged with the two analysts who were working in the city. The appointments were set for the next Saturday.

In Lanigan, the doctor wrote out a report for the school division indicating that I was going on medical leave for mental-health issues. The Director of Education protested the doctor's decision and said he wanted a different doctor's opinion, a doctor that he would choose. It was hard to replace a second-language teacher and a computer teacher, let alone a teacher who could teach both disciplines.

I refused to agree to see another doctor, believing that my doctor's statement was more than enough to meet legal requirements. With me not backing down, the Director told me that I was to leave the school without telling the staff why I was leaving. Mental-health issues needed to be kept as quiet as possible so that the staff wouldn't be upset. Before the school administration could act to stop me, I called a staff meeting and told my friends and colleagues why I was going to be gone. I disclosed as much as I could in the short time before noon break was over.

I also tried to call a student assembly to follow that meeting with the staff, but that was immediately blocked by the principal and the Director, who had just arrived to have me removed from the building. At Marynia's suggestion, I turned to the local newspaper to tell my story to the students and the community. The published story told the community that I would be gone from the community and why I would be gone. For Marynia's sake and Dorian's sake, I didn't want rumours to run rampant. The community deserved the truth. Though I was going to be gone for mental help, Marynia and Dorian would be remaining in the community and they would need the community's support.

The school principal and the Director were angry that I had gone around them directly to the community. The Director told me that I wouldn't be returning to teach in the school anytime in the future, that teachers who burnt out never came back. I had now burnt my bridges with the school division. At that point, I just didn't care. I needed to get help. Neither the Director nor the principal had been in Lanigan long enough to understand the depth of connection that existed between the community and the teachers who had committed to being in their school for the long haul. I owed the community and the teachers, and I needed that community to continue to be there for my family through the tough time that was yet to come.

-

Marynia drove me to Calgary to meet with Zeljko, and Mae, the two analysts I had previously contacted. While the interviews took place, Marynia found me a place to live, a room in a co-op house within walking distance of both offices. The closer location of Mae's house helped me determine which of the two analysts to choose. With that choice made, Marynia persuaded me to buy a laptop computer so that the desktop computer at home would be left for her use. With a new computer, an Internet account was added. Now, we could stay connected. The analytical sessions were set to begin the first week of March.

For the next six months I attended three sessions per week with Mae, focusing on dreams, writing, and using art therapy to help regain psychological balance. I also attended evening seminars and week-end workshops with Zeljko, as I wanted to get a better grasp of what was going on within me from a Jungian psychology perspective. It became a six-month period of full-time self-rescue work with my guides. On the sidelines, I also joined in a Jungian psychology on-line discussion group which was in process of falling apart. I was still invested in life in cyberspace, and took advantage of the on-line group falling apart, to create a new discussion group I called Jung-L.

It wasn't long before the dreams began to tell me that what was working beneath the surface. I knew I was going in the right direction in confronting the darkness and the dangers buried deep within. A dream from the first week in analysis affirmed the risk:

> ... the baby boy is in danger of falling under the wheels of the train ... I try moving forward to save him from certain death, but I lose sight of the boy ... the driver of the LRT sees what is happening, me trying to rescue the boy and the boy slipping towards the wheels ... he begins the slowdown of the LRT ... I feel terrible feeling unable to rescue the boy ... it appears too late to save him as he has disappeared ... the LRT has stopped, and I rush forward and to my amazement find the boy safe ... with a whoop I quickly pick him up, hug him, and give him a kiss ...

I had learned years earlier before changing from psychology to computer-mediated communication master's program, that all the people in dreams are different faces of the dreamer. I was the little boy, the driver, and the ego who works at trying to rescue the little boy. What was being rescued was the inner child, my inner child, who had been abused by parents, other adults, and by a life of chaos.

But it wasn't all positive. There were many, too many, dark shadows that threatened my sanity. The work was leaving me more and more exhausted. I wanted to quit the whole process several times. I was crying for no apparent reason: crying in the middle of the night when sleep refused to come; crying while attempting to write more of my story or while writing down the dreams remembered; crying in the middle of the afternoon when the house was empty; and crying on the long drives to and from my home in Lanigan every second weekend. At those times, I didn't feel like I was getting any better. If anything, I felt worse than ever. Yet, intellectually I knew that this was part of letting go of the ghosts from the past that had been called back from the banished corners of my psyche.

Letting go of the ghosts was one thing, however, giving up authority to my analyst was something else entirely. The more I learned about Jungian psychology, the more I came to understand what Mae was doing and why she was demanding what she did of me. Before too many months had passed, I took what I learned to the on-line discussion group where I began to carve out a Jungian persona. But worse still, was trying to use my limited knowledge to unconsciously sabotage my own process with Mae, to show her that I was still in control.

As I continued working with Mae over the late winter and spring, it began to feel as if I was going over and over the same scripts, again and again; the same stories with changes that didn't seem to lead forward. I felt like a hamster stuck on a wheel going around and round. One of my dreams from the end of March highlighted this feeling:

> ... I am wandering down nature trails searching for a particular path ... searching ... I find the river after crossing sand hills, dunes with bits of grass ... I cross the river using things floating in the river as a raft of sorts ...

> ... I find myself back where I had begun the search and again set off on the quest ... again and again but each time there are variations ... I find myself back in time though still in my present state of age and awareness ... I see a house, part of row-housing ... I'm inside of the house and sense the poverty ... it's small, dark, and in disarray ... it's old and in need of repair ...

... I find myself in the arms of a young woman ... I am caressing her and wanting to possess her sexually ... my hands are under her clothes, touching her skin and sparking a fire of desire within me, a lusting ... she is forbidden fruit and I know it ... I've been here before ... I ache to enter her here in this messy place of poverty ...

The dream was a dark dream. The idea of *forbidden fruit.* What it was from the past that had evoked this part of the dream? I understood the idea of finding myself back in the past, understood the dream was giving me a message I didn't want to hear. I didn't realise it yet, but *forbidden fruit* was going to become a significant part of the healing journey many years later.

My intellect wasn't as powerful as I had once believed. As the analytic process continued, I came to accept that Mae was a needed guide through the inner swamplands. With her guidance, I was able to reclaim most of my life, more than enough to seriously think about returning to a normal life as a teacher and as a husband.

Chapter Fourteen – Zenon Park and Shellbrook

A moment of light in an otherwise darkening world, Shellbrook, 2000.

In the fall of 1998, I returned to teaching in the high school. I was more functional as a teacher than I had been for quite a few years. I continued to make the drive to Calgary for analysis which allowed me to keep my hard-won balance. It wasn't easy to return to the same school and community, especially after exposing my past to that community. It wasn't easy, but it was a vital part of my recovery process.

The greatest challenge was working with the school administration and the Director of Education. Neither of them wanted me back in the school, especially after how I had controlled my exit from the school. Regardless, I had the support of most of the staff which made all the difference, and the School Division Board. These were the people who had been there for me, who had been there for Marynia during the analytic work in Calgary. They were friends as much as they were colleagues.

In March 1999, Mae had heard enough of my constant complaints about the principal and the Director. She challenged me to do something about it, to become the authority rather than complain about it from a safe distance. I had been in the school and the community for twenty years and had only another six years to go to retirement. To jeopardise my career, and to abandon this community for a new one in which I could be the school administrator, was not a decision I could take lightly, it was a decision that needed to have Marynia's support.

The relationship with the Director continued to deteriorate. He was making it harder for me, as well as the school principal, who finally realised that I was doing a good job teaching since my return from analysis in Calgary. The principal apologised to me for contributing to the problem rather than giving support when it had been needed. Yet, is spite of that apology, the principal continued to follow the directives of the Director who wanted me gone from the school.

Fed up, and still angry, I finally took the challenge given to me by Mae. I applied for a position of principal of a different school rather than stay and complain about the principal and Director in Lanigan. It didn't take long for a school to hire me. I was offered the position of principal at a French immersion school in Zenon Park, Saskatchewan. It felt good to be recognised, yet it didn't feel so good to be abandoning the town that had been my home for twenty years.

Getting the job was the easiest part. The hardest part was making the transition from teacher in Lanigan with a family, to living alone in another community as principal, in a different school system. Marynia had invested too much in the community to give it all up without proof that I could succeed with this new role and stick with it. She worried that the pressure would only result in yet another mental crash for me.

I commuted between the two towns at least twice a week for the school year of 1999-2000. At times, Marynia would make the commute to Zenon Park to spend time there with me. She needed to see for herself how I was doing in the school and community. She also needed to figure out if she would be able to fit into that French community should I remain as principal there for the following year. Because of constantly being on the road between Lanigan and Zenon Park, my continuing psychoanalysis with Mae had come to an end.

The challenge of school administration went well. I was valued as the school principal by the staff and students, the community, the Director, and by the other administrators in the school district. The only negatives that emerged were an exacerbation of my environmental allergies, and the fact that the francophone portion of the community was distant and unfriendly to Marynia. She didn't speak any French. Knowing that she wouldn't be able to fit into the French community, and concerned about my allergies, she decided that my staying in Zenon Park wasn't going to happen. If we were going to be together for the following year, I would have to find a position in a different school, in a different community.

And so, began yet another job search. I found a job as principal in Canwood, a larger school in an English-speaking community. Because of few housing options available in the small town, we bought a house in Shellbrook, a larger community which was less than a half hour away on a very good highway. We made the move to Shellbrook in early July 2000. It wasn't an easy move, especially for Marynia who had to give up her community roles and her Emergency Services career. We had spent half a year apart while I was in Calgary, and then a full school year apart. Neither of us did well when separated.

Before the end of the summer, things began to deteriorate at the new school in Canwood, even before the school year was ready to begin. The Director who had hired me, had found a new job in Alberta, and his replacement was a former classmate of mine from university. We hadn't been friends at university, as I had consistently earned higher marks. Despite my having met with all the teachers and having created a teaching plan based on their preferences, someone at the Canwood School had stirred up the teachers to protest their teaching assignments. These were the same assignments that they had asked for in their interviews which only made the situation very confusing for me. The Director wouldn't listen to any explanations I offered. He supported the teachers' demands regardless of the evidence I presented. The timetables had to be redone in less that two days.

While problems at the school and with the new Director began to unfold before the start of the school year, our second child, Natalie, chose to get married in a civil ceremony at our home in Shellbrook. Natalie had chosen a man that made her smile, and that was all that was important. Not yet knowing how the drama with the teachers was unfolding in the background, the September long week-end wedding was a real celebration for Marynia and me. We were overjoyed that our Natalie was marrying a man that she loved, and who loved her in return.

The school year had barely begun when the teachers, with the full support of the Director, began to create the conditions needed to have me removed as principal. Innuendo and vague complaints were treated as facts that needed to be dealt with and fixed. Not knowing what was really going on behind the scenes, I was left to struggle with the constantly shifting situation as best I could. I focused on administrating the school and working with the First Nations community that had been threatening to remove First Nation students from the school.

The parents and elders from the nearby reserve met with me just days before the threatened walkout. Following the meeting, they decided to keep their students in the public school rather than return them to the school on the reserve. I had met with the tribal elder to seal the agreement with a sweet grass ceremony in my office. That decision meant that I could then keep all the teaching staff and not lose any budget as well. I had already built a new teaching timetable assuming a reduced staff at the direction of Director.

Changing the minds of the tribal council was a win-win situation that had the Division School Board applauding my successful efforts. A major problem had been solved. However, the Director became even angrier. Again, as I had at university, I had upstaged him. This time, it was in front of the School Division Board. I hadn't been aware that the issue was about the Director's ego. I still thought that it had to be a combination of my blindness to what I was doing, and something behind the scenes in the community and school.

Since I had admitted to being Métis, and had joined the local Métis association, an additional level of distrust which was then leveled by the Director. That distrust was communicated to the faction agitating for my removal. For the first time in my teaching career, students began to be overtly disrespectful to me. What was said by the teachers and their supporters in the community was the reason for the growing disrespect.

Because of this uncharacteristic turn, I began to doubt myself as a leader and tried even harder to build bridges with the students.

In the community of Shellbrook, where we lived, it was a different story. Both of us had made friends. Marynia had found work in her field, working at the nursing home and at the hospital. I had become an executive member of the local Métis society. For the first time, I no longer felt the need to hide my indigenous roots. We golfed together and made golf friends. The contrast between the community in which I worked and the community in which we lived was like night and day.

In early winter, a formal enquiry was launched by the Saskatchewan Teachers Federation to deal with the complaints they had received about me from the teachers. The Director had contacted the STF to set the process in motion, demanding that a formal enquiry be held. The complaints were treated with seriousness by the STF because of the numbers of people laying the complaints, complaints that were supported by the Director who had added his own complaints to the list of concerns.

As the enquiry unfolded, I was told that I was insensitive to all staff members, and it was suggested that I was sexually inappropriate with the female staff members. No specific examples could be brought forward to substantiate any of the charges laid against me, which made the enquiry difficult for the representatives of the Teachers Federation. All that could be proven was that the atmosphere in the school was extremely toxic.

The mere suggestion of being a sexual threat to the female teachers, without any specifics being brought forward to substantiate the claims, had raced through the community of Canwood. I was judged as guilty even if there weren't any specific acts of sexual misconduct of which I was being accused. For the community, just the hint of potential sexual misconduct was enough to condemn me. They believed the teachers whom they had known, more than the stranger who had become the school's principal. I realised that I was effectively done as a principal in the school. I informed the Director that I was immediately taking stress leave as I couldn't combat the culture of slander in the school and community. He was ecstatic. He had won his war. He immediately banned me from returning to the school with the demand that I hand over the school keys to him.

Not realising that there were other politics operating in the background, I was surprised when the District Board of Education put pressure on the Director to fix the problem. The Division Board had seen what I had done to save the school enrolment and staff numbers, and they had been impressed. So, instead of going on stress leave to finish the school year, I was given the role of principal in Shell Lake which was in the same school division. I had their vote of confidence, but the Director vowed that I wouldn't last at the Shell Lake School.

The four months in the Canwood School had broken my confidence as a teacher with twenty-five years of teaching success. It had broken my confidence as a principal. There were still four and a half years to go until retirement, and that self-confidence would never fully return. Of course, I didn't know that at the time. I assumed that all would be well again once I was in a different school.

I swapped schools with the principal of Shell Lake, the man who had ironically been the choice of the Canwood staff. Finally, I understood what the real agenda was for the staff's abhorrent misbehaviours. It had nothing to do with me. It had everything to do with them getting the principal they wanted for their school.

After an initial period of distrust in Shell Lake, I was working well with staff, students, and the local board. It was a small school and I began to think that it would be the perfect place to finish my career. I found myself teaching more than I had in Canwood. The teaching was rewarding. I introduced new courses at the high school level, improved the school's technology, and soon found myself with a happy staff and student body.

Yet, in contradiction with what was going on in the school, the Director told me that I wouldn't be in the school the following year. No one wanted me to stay at the school, nor anywhere else in the school division. The local school board was surprised and dismayed when I informed them of my search for another school principalship. They thought we had developed a good working relationship together. They were unaware of the Director's comments. The local board hadn't heard any complaints from any of the staff members or from the community. The Director simply wanted me gone. He did offer to give me a glowing recommendation, as long as it was for a principalship in a different school division.

Chapter Fifteen – An Agent of Change

Standing in front of the school waiting to greet my students in
Mortlach, September 2001.

I was fortunate to find another school in a different school
division. The next stop in my career as a principal was in
Mortlach. The new Director, Ivan, who had hired me, told me
that my main task for the coming months was to clean up the
school, to get the teaching staff back on track as
professionals. There had been a culture of relying on student
suspensions to maintain control. That needed to be fixed.
Ivan had fired the last principal against the wishes of the
staff, because she had escalated the use of suspensions. My
real job was to be an agent of change, to change the school
culture.

I had doubts about the job not long after taking the position,
especially when I found out that I was once again facing a
hostile staff and a divided, hostile community. The only
reason I took the job in the first place, was the belief that in
this situation I had the full backing and protection of the

Director of Education and the Division School Board. What I hadn't counted on was being overly sensitised, especially with regards to women because of the experiences at Canwood. This would make my work in the school much more difficult. I tried to please dissidents, rather than confront their bad behaviours. I didn't trust the women teachers enough to ever meet with them while alone in my office. They sensed that weakness. And, they exploited it.

My colleagues administrating other schools in the district, were an ambitious and energetic group of principals and vice-principals. I soon became an integral part of the technology team, which the Director wanted to use to build the reputation of the school division. His vision was to have the school division be the most technologically advanced in the province, if not in the whole of western Canada. I soon found myself thriving in this culture of technological excellence. But, in the background, a different and darker story was beginning to unfold back in Mortlach. I was under attack, an attack that was also targeting the Director.

The Director soon found out that whatever he discussed in my office was heard and communicated to the school staff and to the community, as well as a legal firm. The Director had me relocate the office so that it didn't have a wall shared by the secretary's office, a space that was open to all staff members. The teaching staff and community had engaged lawyers to challenge the Director's, and my right to be administrators. I was fortunate to have the District School Board on side and actively speaking on my behalf to the local school board.

The previous principal, who had been fired, was now a Director of Education in the neighbouring school division. Still bitter about being fired, she was a significant player acting behind the scenes, stirring up the situation. She provided encouragement and advice to the teachers and supporting parents, in their opposition to both myself and the Director, especially against the Director.

While this was going on, I began to work with the students, building a level of mutual respect, especially with those students who had been the target of the previous administrator. They were the first to notice they weren't being unfairly punished. Before I disciplined, I listened and took what was heard into consideration. I mediated and counselled when appropriate. Under the previous administration, it was the school versus the students, especially the students who were not the children of the self-appointed community leaders. That school culture was already starting to become student-centred.

Student suspensions were drastically reduced. Although there were still too many suspensions, in my opinion. From the community and staff points of view, there were drastically too few suspensions. They believed the school was becoming an unsafe environment as a result. In order to change their mindset, I took a role in teaching part-time, as I knew that this was important for both students and teachers. They needed to see the principal as one of them, rather than being a person out of touch and apart from them.

The problem students became less and less of a problem, and soon more than a few of them were in my office for informal counselling. The parents of these 'problem' students soon became my advocates in the community. They felt their children weren't unfairly being targeted anymore. My confidence as a teacher returned. Yet, the problems weren't fixed by any means.

A small portion of the community had asked the Teachers' Federation to revoke my teaching license. This group was composed mainly of the family members of those few teachers openly challenging my presence in the school. They were hoping that impending legal action would somehow make it impossible for me to ever teach or be a principal again. Their primary objective was to get rid of both me and the Director. I was well aware another part of the community, a growing part, was supportive of me. That support group included the town's mayor who had recently become a friend.

Knowing I wasn't alone in the community and that some of the staff were shifting their positions, I began to do the work of rebuilding the school culture using a Jungian approach. With the approval of the Director. I used the book, The Hero's Journey: How Educators Can Transform Schools, to structure the approach that would change the culture of the school. Rather than retreat, I decided to confront the negative culture.

I brought the staff together for a two-day workshop to hammer out a mission statement and a belief statement for the school. They needed the responsibility to collectively shape and own the school's guiding principles. A powerful set of documents emerged, which were then voted upon and accepted, mostly because I had used their own words to craft the documents. Regardless of the results, the staff felt they had been manipulated into making these very public statements about what was needed for a positive school culture. The intensity of their rebellion via their families and friends escalated.

Before winter fully set in, an external group was brought in to evaluate the situation. After numerous questionnaires and interviews, the findings proved that there had been an orchestrated collusion to destroy both the Principal and the Director as administrators, and that it was a collusion that continued to thrive. The external group realised through extensive interviews with the staff, students, and a significant portion of the community, that the campaign had begun before my arrival in the community and that what I did or didn't do while at the school was irrelevant to the group's plan. The Director was furious when he heard the results of the evaluation. He told me to charge forward with the project to reform the school, even if it meant the removal of a few key staff members who were behind the attempted coup.

Because of the support I had been getting from Ivan, Marynia began to think that there was a chance that we wouldn't have to change schools again. She saw me cope with the adversity in the school without having any mental-health setbacks. She was surprised at my equilibrium and focus.

By the time spring arrived, one teacher had been fired and another teacher had been transferred. More changes for the following school year were promised by the Director. Over the second half of the year, there were fewer student suspensions. There was real movement in the school's culture, real change, but not enough to have me feel confident enough to want to stay and endure more of this concerted opposition. I had willingly taken on the role of bad cop, and now what the school needed a good cop.

I felt a need to move on to a new school. With the Director's reluctant blessing. Another job search began.

I hadn't yet figured it out, but I wasn't ever going to be comfortable as the authority figure in any school. I just was not capable of dealing with the politics of a community school. I believed in playing by rules of fairness, something that made me an easy target for those who had no qualms about getting their way without regard to fairness or rules. For them, all that mattered were their agendas. I believed that most teachers also wanted to play by the rules, in a school with a positive culture.

Chapter Sixteen – Elrose

The last year at Elrose Composite School, October 2004.

It was a relief for both Marynia and me when I found a school principalship in the Eston-Elrose School Division. The fear of being alone with a female staff member continued to influence my relationships with the new staff. I was careful, very careful in talking with the female staff members. I would always have the vice-principal, a woman, sit in on all such meetings. It became apparent quickly, that the staff was basically satisfied with me as their new principal, as they felt I was an improvement over the one who had just been transferred to another school in the division.

Having been burnt in previous schools over the past two years, I began to wonder when, not if, my professional life would begin falling apart in this new school. Would I make it through the year? Would I be able to make it through the next three years until retirement? There was no rush to buy a house, even though the house we had bought in Shellbrook had finally been sold. I needed to prove to both Marynia and myself that I could stay in the school longer than one year.

In the fall of 2002, I began my tenure as principal in Elrose. Marynia joined the local volunteer ambulance association. The year went well, a lot better than had been expected. There were problems of course, as there are always problems in a school where teachers and students and parents end up in assorted conflicts. Most of the issues were minor and easily resolved.

What was different about the school in Elrose was the belief by students and staff that education was important, and that respect was the best way to get that education. The students worked hard and played hard. Most of the teachers had no reservations about putting in the extra time needed for coaching, leading student activities, and tutoring. Perhaps most important in the process, was the belief the community had in their school. In a way, it was as if I had finally found a school to match the school I had left in Lanigan.

At the start of the second school year in Elrose, with everything going well, Marynia and I finally decided to buy the house which we had been renting. There had been no indications of problems bubbling in the background. We had made friends in the community. And, we were now grandparents to a fourth grandson, the second child of Natalie, living in North Dakota.

Near the end of the second year, the decision for tenure was being considered, I was told by the Director, Mike in early May that all was well and that I would be receiving confirmation of my tenure in the school as principal before the end of the school year. I had read the Director's final report and it was only a matter having the Division Board ratify the Director's report. Then, it all began to fall apart.

Just weeks before the meeting, I had to call in the Teachers' Federation because of a serious set of allegations made by a few female students against a male teacher who was new to the school. Things moved so fast behind the scenes that I was caught by surprise when less than a week later, the Teachers Federation supported that teacher's dismissal requested by the Director. Before the young teacher left, he visited me at home and told me I was next on the chopping block, that I had serious enemies both inside and outside of the school.

The teacher had spoken the truth though I didn't know it. My days as principal of the Elrose school were numbered. I had assumed that the words of the dismissed teacher were nothing but the teacher's bitterness at being fired.

The next Division Board meeting resulted in the Board not accepting the Director's report and demanding that I be placed on a strict one-year extended probation with a wide variety of areas of concern being raised. Those areas had not been noted as concerns in the report the Director had given to the Board. Someone, or more than one person, had a vendetta. Whoever that person was had power and influence with the Board.

The Director retired at the end of the school year and a new Director took his place, a man I knew well and whom I considered as a friend. I believed that with the new Director's support, things were going to turn out much better. However, behind the scenes, politics ruled. With the new Director fearing his own job loss if he didn't follow what he was told to do, the support never materialised.

In that third year in December 2004, with most of the school year left to meet the targets set by the School Board, I was told that I would not be able to continue as principal in the school, or as a principal at any other school in the division for the 2005-2006 school year. Despite the six months left to address the issues, several of which had been dealt with, the final decision had already been made. If I refused to resign, I would be demoted to a teaching position to be in a different school within the division.

It didn't matter to me anymore. I had reached the goal of being able to retire, but I still wanted to continue as principal in the school. I was devastated. I couldn't understand what had happened. The local school board, the community, and the staff had supported and respected me and were just as confused and upset as I was. Every voice told me that the school was running better than it had for quite some time. It was only at this time the pieces began to fall into place letting me know that it was again politics behind the scene that were forcing the issue of my retirement. The reasons that had nothing to do with me as a person or as a principal. I began to suffer from depression.

Marynia and I went to Cuba for the two-week Christmas break in 2004. We both knew that this was the end of my teaching career, my last year as a teacher. I would retire, rather than be humiliated by being demoted and transferred. The will power to search for yet another school to hire me as their principal, didn't exist, nor was it an option for Marynia. I had wanted to remain in education for at least another five years, in this school and in this community. Elrose had been adopted as my home community. I now felt a deep sense of shame for having failed.

The nightmares that had vanished not long after the analysis in Calgary in 1998, returned while we were in Cuba. A mixture of alcohol, a deep sense of failure, and self-blame saw me return to physical and mental self-abuse. Both of us feared what was again happening – I was beginning to have another breakdown.

In the daylight hours, I found myself inexplicably stripping off clothes and sunbathing on the balcony of the suite in Cuba. I had never dared this much nudity since the early years of our marriage other than with our long-standing tradition of night-time, skinny-dipping escapades, a family affair. Neither of us risked confronting the issue of my nudity in Cuba.

The re-emergence of nudity in my life, was an unconscious response to the pressing shadows within. At first, I was being nude within the confines of the suite following a long morning walk along the beach, something that didn't cause Marynia much stress. As she watched me lying on my stomach on the bed, she placed a flower on me and then took a photo, an innocent photo that was meant for humour, comic relief. This was the man she loved.

I took photos of Marynia on the same bed, beautiful images with her smiling. Then, with her permission, I took photos of the two of us together which again captured her Caribbean happiness. Aside from scattered moments of darkness, Cuba gifted us with warmth, flowers, and time. My own eyes revealed a brooding, haunted spirit. Marynia's photo of me, had been the first nude image taken of me in my life, unlike the numerous times over the years that I had taken nude photos of her. I was surprised when Marynia agreed to having nude photos of the two of us together, something that had never happened in the past.

Nudity had just returned in a way that was different from the stolen moments at an isolated beach or while night-time skinny dipping. As in my youth, I was subconsciously awakened to the healing powers of the sun. It wasn't long before I tried to take my nudity onto the sheltered balcony of our resort suite. The need for nudity was an unconscious need. Unknown to either Marynia or me, was the role that nudity would come to play in my journey through the darkness and the storms that lay ahead of us. And, as in the past, there was an occasional night skinny dip. The feel of the water and the cool air awakened something within me. It was as if a long-forgotten switch had been turned back on.

Once school started up following the Christmas break, I gave my notice to the school board for retirement. I had completed thirty years in public education. I was finished with the politics of administration in public education. I now had no dreams for the future. I had no sense of what was to happen next in the spring of 2005 as I put in the last few months of my career in the community school. My ambition had died.

Part Three

Swamplands of the Soul

"An old saying has it that religion is for those who are afraid of going to Hell; spirituality is for those who have been there. Unless we are able to look at the existential discrepancy between what we long for and what we experience, we will remain forever in flight, or denial, or think of ourselves as victims, sour and mean-spirited to ourselves and others."

James Hollis, Swamplands of the Soul: New Life in Dismal Places

Chapter Seventeen – Side Stepping to Avoid the Shadow

A fresh start at Fond du Lac School, September 2005.

"Bob," Marynia began what she knew was going to be a difficult topic. "Do you think that maybe you could find a new teaching job on a reserve or in the north where we began? Since you'll have a pension, we could keep our house here and likely add to our savings in the process. I know that doing nothing after retirement will be a disaster for you."

"I guess it's possible," I responded with very little enthusiasm. "I really haven't thought about what I'm going to do next."

131

"I know that," Marynia replied with more than a bit of exasperation. "You're walking around as if you're a zombie. We can't live like this. It has to change."

"What made you think of me teaching on a reserve?" I asked, feeling the pressure that came with her reaching her limits.

"That was your original intention as a teacher. After all, you did major in Native Studies and work in the north for more than a few years.

"And?" I probed knowing that there was more that Marynia had to tell me.

"And I saw these jobs advertised," she replied as she showed me the ads for a principal position in two reserve schools.

I looked at the two advertisements. The one for Fond-du-Lac Reserve, immediately grabbed my attention. Marynia was right. Here was a school, a large school, not too far from Uranium City. It was close to where I had begun my career.

I looked at it again and then at Marynia, "Would you be willing to go with me if I got this job?"

"Of course, silly. Just don't ask me to sell our home here in Elrose."

Since I didn't have to worry about money anymore, being assured of a pension, all I needed was something to do that would make me feel good about myself, something that would give me a sense of purpose. With my experience and education, I needed to be back in a school.

-

In April 2005, I applied for and was given the job of principal and Director of Education for the Fond-du-Lac Reserve school. In early May, I was flown into Fond du Lac to meet with the Chief and the staff of the school. I met with teachers who were to remain for the next school year. I gave each person a separate and private interview hoping to learn what they needed and wanted for going forward. In a strange way, it was like coming home as I met a former student from my first school in Camsell Portage, the same youth, Garnet Stelle, who had lived with us in Buffalo Narrows, and for a short time in Saskatoon. My impressions of Fond du Lac were very, very favourable.

It didn't take long once the school year began, before an intense political storm began to stir up within the school. The staff was fearful of the idea that the principal would also be their evaluator as Director of Education. They wanted someone else to be Director. At the least, they wanted an outsider appointed for teacher evaluation, someone at a safe distance. The Chief refused to listen to their complaints and encouraged me to do what was necessary to transform the school into a place that was less violent and more accountable to the educational needs of the students. He had me begin with double checking the teaching credentials of all the teachers, which led to the removal of a Special Education teacher who had no teacher training, nor a university degree. The teacher hired in replacement was qualified. That act seemed to ease the tensions that had been growing between me and some of the staff. I had just protected them because they were real teachers.

Everything appeared to be going well with life as a principal and director, especially in terms of my relations with the band council and the chief. I was doing the necessary work to make their vision for education on the reserve become a reality. I attended formal meetings of the band council, as well as meetings with the Prince Albert Grand Council (PAGC). The relationship with the Federal government that autumn was on the verge of resolving critical issues on many reserves, especially in education. Expectations were high throughout the fall and into the beginning of the winter in 2005, because of the proposed legislation that was aimed at fixing the Indian Act.

Marynia had taken on the role of being a substitute teacher for the school as there were no substitute teachers to be found. She had obtained a temporary teacher's certificate from the province so that I would be legally able to have her work as a substitute teacher. If a teacher was sick in the past, students were sent home until the teacher was ready to return. Since Marynia had experience teaching in the emergency health field, I felt that she could fill in the role of substitute teacher quite well. It wasn't long before the school staff agreed with me. She was soon seen as a valued team member.

In October, Marynia flew off to North Dakota for the birth of our fifth grandson while I kept busy with meetings and administration. At Christmas time, I finally got to meet the latest of my grandsons when all our children and grandchildren came home to Elrose for a family reunion. My life and work appeared to be back on track.

Following the Christmas break, towards the end of January, the mood on the reserve took a sharp turn for the worse. All the work at the PAGC with the Federal government looked to have been wasted. There was going to be a change in government and the new Prime Minister, Stephen Harper, had a drastically different philosophy in dealing with First Nations. The local council lost faith in the Chief and began to agitate for their personal agendas. The reserve divided the community into family-factions. The Chief didn't have the power he needed, in this climate of internal conflict, to continue driving his vision for the school and community.

It was in this climate of renewed agitation on the reserve, when a charge of harassment was levelled by a young, white female teacher against another teacher, a male who was First Nations. I listened carefully to both sides. I found myself trying to protect the young female teacher, who was terrified and ready to quit because of her fear. I didn't want to again be in search of another teacher. The young man turned the conflict into a racial issue rather than a harassment issue. On the advice of the Chief, I put the male teacher on paid leave until the matter could be resolved by the band council. They would investigate the charges of racism levelled by the male teacher and of harassment by the female teacher.

Following an in-camera meeting, I was told to reinstate the male teacher and to be careful about which side I chose to support in the future. The meeting ended with me being told to stay in the teacherage while the committee considered what should be done next. To me, it felt like I was being put under house arrest by the committee.

Following the meeting, after which I was threatened by two of the councillors who were political enemies of the chief, I made an immediate decision to leave on the next flight leaving from the reserve's airport. I honestly feared for my and Marynia's safety. Neither of us needed to be immersed in the storm that was brewing on the reserve.

We had a home and economic security back in Elrose. I managed to keep my intentions quiet until I got a ride taking our belongings to the airport and for the flight out to Saskatoon. Upon arrival at the airport, someone alerted the Chief. He arrived just as we were about to board the plane. It was too late for the chief to change my mind. I was leaving even though the Chief's promised that it would all work out well. I knew that it was a promise beyond his power to keep. I left the reserve formally taking stress leave.

-

Back home in Elrose we let people know that I had finished my assignment at Fond du Lac. At Marynia's suggestion, we wasted no time in planning a quick vacation to Cancun, Mexico with a neighbouring couple, Faye and Cameron. The week in Mexico should have been a great vacation given the perfect weather, but as in Cuba, I found myself once again slipping into a depression. At times I would stay behind in the room while Marynia went out with our friends. I claimed having a headache. In the privacy of our resort room, I once again removed my clothing. It took a few days of solitude and decompression before I could finally shake off enough of the depression to enjoy the days that remained. In the background, behind my smiles, I again judged myself as a failure.

Back home, we agreed that I just wasn't cut out for the politics of educational leadership. The fact that we didn't need the money only made the decision to not apply to another school that much easier. Regardless, I was adrift. I still needed to do something. I was too young to retire to a rocking chair.

It was then that I remembered the idea of teaching at a university, an idea which I first voiced as a high school student in grade ten in Ottawa. It was a dream that couldn't happen without returning to study for a doctorate, an option I wasn't ready to consider. Then, I remembered the posters I had seen on the bulletin boards at the university, advertising for teachers in foreign countries. Perhaps this is the way I would be able to reach that dream from forty years earlier.

Inspired with the possibilities, I began to search for the next best thing, teaching English at a university in another country, a job which didn't demand a PhD. I set my hopes for China, a place I had been interested in since I was a teenager. At that time, I had read about Pierre Trudeau's time in China. I found several advertisements for university jobs in China and applied for one in a city called Changzhou, a city not far from Shanghai. I sent an e-mail to the university and received a quick response asking for a resume, photos and a copy of my passport. They replied the next day telling me that I had a job with them and that I needed to get a visa and sign the contract which they would e-mail.

After talking with Marynia about the job offer, I asked about a job for her at the university, telling them it would be the only way I would take a job with them. Marynia was graciously offered a position as a teacher of conversational English.

Chapter Eighteen – China Part One

VIPs on the Great Wall of China, April 2008.

The China adventure was just that, a real adventure. For the next two years Marynia and I navigated through the customs and rituals of university academic life and as expats in China. We were treated as V.I.P.s and we thrived.

There were problems of course, normal problems that had nothing to do with my life falling apart, or of being haunted by the ghosts of the past. The problems mostly concerned issues of communication and of cultural adjustment. It helped that I had been a teacher and was good at teaching. None of the other foreigners hired by the university had been teachers, so they based their teaching on how they had been taught in North America or Australia. It didn't take long for the university to offer me a greater level of respect in comparison to the others. In their eyes they saw me as a master teacher who had a lot to teach even the Chinese instructors who taught English as a Second Language.

With this higher level of appreciation, my ego was stroked. *'Finally,'* I thought, *'people are getting to see the real me.'* It was the first time in my life that I had experienced this level of respect. Interestingly, but not surprisingly, with that praise and respect I worked harder and with more creativity to deserve it.

It didn't take us long to venture out of the city to visit more distant places, trusting to my planning skills and intuition. Before the arrival of winter, we had visited Beijing, Shanghai, and Suzhou, cities that had a long history with which I was familiar. By the end of the first term we decided to spend the six-week term break in the sub-tropical south of China. Changzhou City didn't have central heating and it was very damp and cold.

We went to Sanya, a place which was China's version of Hawaii. It wasn't long before my clothes came off as I sat on the condo's balcony to absorb the rays of the sun. After an initial tension and resistance, Marynia conceded to this need for nudity, wondering what it was about tropical places, which ended up with me being nude. I couldn't answer her questions though I knew that there had to be something deep within me that compelled this strange behaviour.

The six weeks passed quickly and left both of us feeling glad that we had chosen this unique Chinese experience, especially when the condo's owner, a lady from Shanghai, joined us for many forays into the Hainan Island culture. We returned to Changzhou rested and ready to begin a second term at the university.

The second term saw our performances as teachers improve. Chinese teachers began sitting in on some of our classes to see how lessons were taught. Both Marynia's and my students had given us the highest ratings of any expat teachers. During this second term, our neighbours from Elrose, Faye and Cameron, the same couple who had spent time in Mexico with us the year before, came to visit for two weeks. They got to share in the classes, daily life experiences, and our Chinese friends. I continued riding an emotional high through the rest of the school term.

When the next national holiday came in May, we travelled, again on our own, to Xi'an. We wanted to see the Terracotta Warriors and the famed walled inner city. By the end of June, we were both relieved and excited to go home to Canada for the summer. We signed a contract for the next school year with a significant pay raise. It was time to unwind, to slow down and get our bearings back at home before Dorian's wedding. Our youngest was getting married during the August long weekend.

A summer to unwind, soon changed into a summer of constant movement, as we tried to recapture the months of lost time with children, grandchildren, and extended family. By the time we needed to leave and return to China, I was wound up tight. Without realising it, I had sacrificed too much needed alone time. And as in the past, I had continued to place the needs of others before my needs.

There had been opportunities for me to take time-outs for solitude and silence, but I consistently passed on them believing that to take that time was nothing but an act of selfishness. There would be a cost to pay for not taking care of my psychological needs. But this was the furthest thing from my mind.

The second year began where the first had left off. If the first year saw us treated like VIPs, the second year we had risen even higher in the university's esteem. We had made the local newspapers on occasions which led to all sorts of business opportunities and guest appearances for which we were paid exorbitant fees. We were minor celebrities.

Marynia and I spent the autumn break taking a riverboat cruise tour of the Three Gorges Dam along the Yangtze

River. The voyage exceeded our expectations. The breadth of the country and its diversity began to teach both of us just how little we really knew about other countries beyond what the mass media had taught us. What we thought we knew was often incorrect.

The end of the first term arrived quickly. We chose to spend four weeks of the winter term break in India. We had already decided that this would be our last year teaching in China and that it would be only sensible to visit India which was nearby rather than to risk never seeing that country. Our decision to make this the last year was because we were missing too much in the lives of our grandchildren.

The reality of India shocked both Marynia and me. There was nothing we had heard or experienced which could have prepared us for the chaotic, churning, and messy reality of India. For the first time I experienced real culture shock. New Delhi was an overwhelming nightmare. The nightmare continued into the next day when I looked out the hotel window at dawn to see people sitting on a massive garbage heap, injecting drugs into their emaciated and grimy bodies. A few hours later, that first morning, we entered a different India, the India I had learned about over the years, the India of history and culture. It was as if the country had a split personality, a Doctor Jekyll and Mr. Hyde personality. We got to see the best and worst of what it was to be a human in India.

It was a relief when we flew to the southwest of India to spend the last twelve days of our break on the beaches of Goa. Again, we were in a tropical paradise, at the edges of the Indian Ocean. This time, there was no instances of nudity. The photos taken during these last days tell a beautiful story, but it wasn't the full story. Something was once again stirring within me, stirring like a cancer threatening to return to life. The return to teaching in Changzhou temporarily silenced that stirring.

A month into the second term, I went to Shanghai to see an uncle, my mother's younger brother, Bob. It was a day where I took time to show my uncle around the city which had become quite familiar to me. Strangely, there was an undercurrent of tension between the two of us that I didn't understand at the time. But it wasn't long after when I realised that he had reminded me of his father, the man who had sexually molested me when I was a teenager. It was an unfair response to my uncle, as he had never showed the least indication of being like his father in that manner. He did look like his father, and that was enough as far as activating a trigger is concerned.

Our first child, Nola and her family came to spend two weeks with us in China. As before when our neighbours had visited the spring before, we shared our life in Changzhou, with side excursions to Beijing and Xi'an.

When Nola and her family departed at the beginning of April, it was hard to get back into the routines of teaching and evaluation as the end of the term approached, especially as Marynia and I had not signed contracts to come back to teach in Changzhou at the university. Our China adventure was ending. Without China to keep my ego centred, I began to worry, *'What am I going to do now?'*

As the term drew closer to the end, the pull of going home brought an end to a slight dip into depression. Excitement took its place. Three of our grandchildren and our second daughter, Natalie, would be waiting for us at the airport in Saskatoon. It had been a long nine months since we had last seen her and her children.

Chapter Nineteen – Swamplands in Mexico

In the swamplands of the Yucatan near Chuburna, Mexico, March 2009.

Back home in Canada, life became another busy round of family and friends. The energy levels surged and surged, as I was constantly surrounded by family for the first six weeks back home. When the house finally became quiet, I set to work repairing the patio deck. I unconsciously knew I needed to keep busy. Marynia, like me, had also found ways to keep busy as she got involved with a Women's Build project with one of our neighbours, travelling to Saskatoon to help construct a house.

In September, we began another round of visiting family which included me flying on my own to British Columbia to visit my mother. It seemed that no sooner had one journey ended when it was time to head out in yet a different direction for another journey. It was as if we were both, unconsciously avoiding being alone at home. It didn't take much of an excuse to find someone else to visit. As life eventually began to slow down in the late stages of autumn. we decided to book a three-month winter stay in Mexico.

By the time November 2008 arrived, we took another road trip to see Marynia's brother, Maksym, who was experiencing the onset of Alzheimer's. Then with that visit over, we were off again to visit another set of grandchildren, and then another set of grandchildren, then our son Dorian and his new wife, before returning home. We finished off the year with everyone coming to our Elrose home to celebrate Christmas. Sometime during all of this busy-ness, I had set up a blog site which was to focus on Jungian psychology and photography.

In January 2009, we flew off to spend three months in Yucatan, Mexico. I began to wonder, '*Are we running? If so, what are we running away from? Or, was this rush to Mexico simply a well-reasoned plan to enjoy sunshine and warm temperatures during the coldest part of a Canadian winter?*' Both Marynia and I knew we were running away from confronting something, we just didn't know what that something was.

We arrived in Chuburna, a very small village in the Yucatan province of Mexico. When we saw of our winter home at the southern edge of the Gulf of Mexico, we knew we had made a good choice. It was a world away from the bustle of Cancun, where we had stayed for a week only three years earlier with Faye and Cameron, our friends in Elrose. Both of us were slow to begin exploring beyond the paths we walked for the first few weeks. We finally took time to immerse ourselves in interpersonal quietness, something we both needed. With waves as background mood music, it was as if we were living a meditative life. Finally, we began to relax. It was the first time in years since we found ourselves alone without the distraction of others and activities. And, for the most part, it was all good.

However, being alone together and wondering what to do, what to say to each other to fill the long hours began to stir things within both of us. We were both out of our natural elements of career, family, friends and community. There were just the two of us. Even life in China had somehow managed to fill most of our time with work, students, friends, and curious Chinese people. There was always something to do, someplace to go when the silence became too much. So, we began to do what we had always done in the past, we went exploring. We walked for hours in every possible direction. Engaging in the outer world, kept the inner voices quiet.

There was a difference this time for me. The difference focused on a change in the filters used by my unconscious in selecting subjects and their presentation with my camera. There was a noted focus on things broken and abandoned and feminine, the power of the feminine. One photo I took of Marynia had her walking through a set of poles, set into the water, with her hands uplifted. A flock of seagulls appeared to be obeying her command to fly from their roosts on the posts. Somehow, I had captured the image of a goddess, a magical image. This goddess was the woman I had married. I saw her at that moment as a Magical Other.

We came across the ruins of an old stone building only steps away from the sea, not too distant from our casa. An old, dead skeleton of a tree stood between the ruins and the beach. As my usual habit, I took photos and wrote blog posts to go with the photos. In one such post I exposed more than information of the scene, it was the opening scene for a journey of self-exploration that would continue for years into the future.

> *"The roots of the tree are found at the beach's edge, where the brush meets the sand, only metres away from the seashore. Like the ruins which are out of view, the tree is stripped bare, exposed to the core. I*

identify with this tree and somehow that is a bit troublesome. What if I were stripped bare of all the masks, all the ruses and illusions created by my conscious and unconscious self?" [January 15, 2009] I had found myself resisting what was appearing. I typically focused on staying undercover – under the radar. I tried hard to prevent my inner self from becoming exposed and vulnerable. It became a battle of control, self-control. *'Who would win the battle, soul or ego?'* I had worked too hard in the past to achieve psychological wellness. That work had been done and there was no way I was going to go back down that road again.

Back at the casa, a place that had become home, we frequently found ourselves retreating into the house during the evenings to escape the strong, cold winds coming off the water, winds that forced us to close the shutters to keep out the salt spray. Inside the casa, I retreated quietly into myself and became increasingly self-critical. I felt I was unworthy of this beautiful woman sitting next to me.

I then realised that buried somewhere deep within me was a darkness that would eventually challenge both of us in the years ahead. I began to doubt that we would hold together when that darkness emerged. So, I fought the darkness, hiding behind forced smiles and a fierce determination to focus more on being present. And, I continued to write:

"I also sense that the tree is an inner self that refuses to be contained by the artificial walls that we build to protect our sense of self, an insecure self that will beg others for positive affirmation. Try as hard as one wants, cracks will appear in the façade, our insecurities will slip out as unconscious contents so that we aren't even aware of the cracks. In the end, we wonder, "What the hell has just happened?" [February 5, 2009]

As February passed in a flurry of activity with Mardi Gras in Merida, and a road trip to Uxmal with our next-door neighbour and one of her American friends; we ventured off the beaten trails of Chuburna to wander at the edges of the local mangrove swamps. While walking along the edges of the swamp, it was as though I had found myself in an all too familiar place, a malodorous place that held dangers unseen beneath the surface of the water.

At times, I would wander off alone with the camera. On sunny days I would stop behind an old abandoned building near the sea and sit in the shelter of a wall, facing the sun. I just wanted to soak in the heat of the sun, to feel myself being cooked. Then, on one such day during our final month in Mexico, ensuring I was hidden by a dune on one side and the wall on the other so that passing beach walkers couldn't see me, I stripped off my clothing, and bared my body to the sun. For a few minutes, I was fully vulnerable. Under the intense rays of sunshine, the darkness I had sensed at the edges of my mind, began to recede allowing me to breath. The dawning of realisation that nudity was healing me, shocked me.

It was the beginning of a new chapter in my life, a very difficult chapter that would test my sanity and my relationship with Marynia. I was turning again to nudity, unconsciously, as I had turned to nudity when I had been a teenager, to stay sane and to cope. I retreated into quiet country spaces to heal, to escape the hungry ghosts of the past. And now, I was turning once again to the role of nudity as part of my journey of healing.

-

The mangrove swamplands called me. I was getting more and more depressed as the final weeks in Mexico passed. It seemed that the only moments of some sort of peace within me, were when I found myself alone in the swamplands near the casa, or when I was nude in the sunshine. I psychologically knew I was once again on the edges of darkness. I unconsciously knew that I was going to have to make a journey through that darkness at some point in the future. I though back the words Carl Gustav Jung used to explain what was going on within me:

> "*One does not become enlightened by imagining figures of light, but by making the darkness conscious.... For our own sake we have to explore the darkness, or we cannot proceed with our lives. The task of midlife is not to look into the light, but to bring light into the darkness.*"

Back at the casa, I had created tension between myself and Marynia. I had begun to find ways to be nude within the casa, and beside the casa where I could still be in the sunshine and yet be protected from the eyes of others. My nudity became a source of conflict. Yet, it seemed the more I tried to repress this need to avoid these conflicts, the more agitated and irrational I became.

Not wanting to risk our marriage, I began to take nudity away from the casa and into the swamplands. I would be alone out there walking in shallow water. My intuition and gut told me that I had work to do there in the swampland, work that could no longer be postponed. I didn't have a family to raise anymore, or a career to attend to anymore. I found these words by James Hollis, an American Jungian analyst and author:

> "... *there is no sunlit meadow, no restful bower of easy sleep; there are rather swamplands of soul where nature, our nature, intends that we live a good part of the journey, and from whence many of the most meaningful moments of our lives will derive. It is in the swamplands where soul is fashioned and forged, where we encounter not only the gravitas of*

life, but its purpose, its dignity and its deepest meaning."

As I wandered through the swamplands, naked, or when I hid behind the dunes unclothed, I had opened a Pandora's Box within me, setting in motion a long and twisting journey of soul recovery.

Yet, it wasn't all darkness. Most of the days were, good days filled with the sunshine. The problem was that the mere existence of those occasional dark days worried both of us, as we had lived through very dark times in the nineties when I had ended up in Calgary for analysis. I was almost sixty years old and retired. Midlife with its crisis had long passed. These years were supposed to be our golden years, not about a return to darkness.

As the end of our stay in Mexico approached, I took another photo, an image of a broken road through the swampland. The work had begun, though I continued to resist it as much as I could. Eventually I conceded resisting, hoping to save my sanity. I was being cooked under the heat of the sun; and in the process, changing. I managed to capture that feeling in one of my blog posts that featured the same photo:

> *"The alchemical work that is in progress while I am here in Mexico is being flooded with so many images that it makes sense to me that it is all about change. I don't know yet if that is good or bad in terms of where I have been and where I am going.... the transformation is not necessarily going to be gentle. The journey looks to be rough and solitary. It can't be any other way. So, I wait and wonder . . ."* [March 25, 2009]

On the fifth of April, we returned to our home on the prairies.

Chapter Twenty – Cooked in Costa Rica

The pull of the ocean in Costa Rico,
the pull to the unconscious, February 2010.

We arrived back at home a few days before Easter. Life quickly slipped back into the normal routines of family, friends and community. There was one new activity, a photography-book project. The objective was to complete a photography book in thirty days. The book was called, Tunnel Vision. I raced through the project only to challenge myself with the completion of a second full book, Discovering the Hero Within, during the same time frame – two photography books in a thirty-day period. I reflected on the idea of the tunnel on the blog site.

"Tunnel vision is part of my life, part of my journey.
Thinking more about tunnel vision, I realised that we

*are all wandering through this earth dimension with
tunnel vision, limited by our shadow, limited by how
little of the personal and collective unconscious that
we have yet faced. Tunnel vision limits not only our
sense of 'self' but also our knowledge of 'other'.*
[April 11, 2009]

Contrary to outer appearances, I was once again engaged in a
disappearing act, disappearing into my own tunnel. My focus
had turned to the outer world, away for paying attention to
what was going on within me. I was doing my best to wear a
smile and be the man others needed and loved. The last thing
I wanted to happen was to once again sink into another
depression.

By the time summer arrived, both books had been completed,
travels to visit grandchildren, time do some basement
renovations, and the playing of numerous games of golf left
me exhausted. It was during this state of fatigue, more
psychological than physical, that we returned to visit
Maksym who showed increasing signs of distress because of
Alzheimer's.

A return home following this visit had me rethink my
relationship with my children. I had been writing quite a bit
about father-complexes and masculinity over the preceding
months on the blog site, and the idea of how the sins of the
father get visited upon the children. I had a lot to think about
in terms of how my being wounded in childhood had in turn
wounded those that followed me.

*"I wonder if the sins of the maternal grandfather get
visited upon their grandsons. Somehow, I think they
do in a curious way, through his daughter to her son
– me ... I will dare to begin writing the story of my
father, his father, and myself. This will be a gift to my
son, as well as my daughters and grandchildren."*
[July 4, 2009]

Where did this resolve come from? Likely, it had sprung from a task that had been left unfinished. I had had issues with men in my life –father, maternal grandfather, and an assortment of adult males who had been authority figures such as priests and administrators in schools and other places of employment. Whatever the reasons, my intention to write the story for my children was abandoned.

Writing was kept simple. Life was full, I was fully engaged in outer life. Following my sixtieth birthday, some inner disquiet began to stir, a feeling I captured in a blog post which began with a quotation:

> *"While we might on some days prefer to simply be happy carrots, relieved of our urgencies, our anxieties and impossible desires, we also suffer greatly when we are not living the life which the psyche wishes us to live. Such existential bad faith will always demand some payment – in the body, in our relationships, in our disturbing dreams, or in the burden our children will have to carry for us."*
> *[James Hollis]*

> *"Like most people, I beat back the urges, the voices, and dreams. Like others, I then have to pay the price in terms of my body. Sleep becomes more difficult and the dreams seem to be taking on a louder voice in an attempt to have me recognize them. I don't want to go there. Instead of recording the dreams and thinking about them. The disquietude within is simmering. I don't want to go there. Why can't I be a happy carrot?"* [July 26, 2009]

Plans were made in the late summer to head south to Costa Rica for the winter

-

The rush to discover the treasures of Costa Rica was in stark contrast to the gradual explorations we had experienced in the Yucatan, Mexico. My camera was kept busy capturing all sorts of interesting images. When we settled into a condo in Playa Jaco, we spent a lot of time exploring the area. It took almost two weeks before we finally began to relax and establish new patterns of living in Costa Rica. The Pacific Ocean captured our attention as we headed out almost every evening to watch the sunset, hypnotised by the colours of Costa Rican sunsets.

It was at this time, two weeks into this paradise, when a return of disquietude began to appear within me. The heat of the sun had begun to affect me. Not aware of the darkness that was beginning to seep out, I was surprised as another conflict with Marynia surfaced. She had finally recognised what was happening. She had been down this road before and she was becoming more and more anxious about my mental health, and angry with me for turning the paradise of Costa Rica into Hell.

As the conflicts reappeared, I once again took refuge in stripping off clothing. In behind the studio was a tiny, private walled yard just big enough to use as a private sunbathing area. It wasn't long before this private time became needed more and more. I was very agitated when I couldn't get that private, healing time.

Nudity was becoming more and more of an issue between us. I was struggling. *'Why do I need to be nude?'* It was in the middle of this struggle that saw me take the nudity out from the private enclosure and into the condo itself. I had taken nudity into our shared space. Coming to realise that Marynia's only place of normality was within the tiny condo, I tried harder to keep my clothing on when she was in the condo. My efforts failed as they always seemed to fail. *'What kind of a husband am I not to give her what she needed from me?*' Marynia hadn't denied me the right to be nude; she only asked for boundaries for her own well-being.

Near the end of the first month in Jaco, I took a photo which was then Photoshopped into a photo of a full moon. The result was called *the man in the moon* and placed it on the blog site. It was the second nude photo of me that had ever been taken. The first had been taken by Marynia in Cuba in December 2004. In the post with the photo, *the man in the moon*, I wrote:

> "*Being transparent, allowing the unconscious contents to inform consciousness so that we have the courage to cease being desperately straight-jacketed. . . The image of the Vitruvian Man is all about wholeness ... the presentation of the Vitruvian Man as a nude by Leonardo da Vinci, is all about transparency, about stripping away of masks and being able to see the true man, vulnerable and yet powerful for all vulnerability.*" [January 29, 2010]

While I resisted the emergence of nudity into my life, Marynia accepted the nudity as long as it was set within boundaries. She saw the differences in me when I risked sunbathing and when I resisted sunbathing. I finally heard her and began to trust a bit more in the process as she spoke positively about me keeping nudity in its proper place. She gave me permission to be nude. I took this permission and relaxed while in the condo enclosure, without worrying about her getting angry and perhaps even leaving me. I had her permission. Yet, I didn't realise that it wasn't only her permission that was needed, I hadn't learned to give myself permission. A mother-complex had intruded into our relationship.

I continued to read and to write. It helped me gained a bit more self-authority as I read the words written by Daryl Sharp, a Jungian analyst and author:

"Work on yourself and a good relationship will follow. You can either accept who you are and find a relationship that fits, or twist yourself out of shape and get what you deserve."

Therein lay the problem. Would the relationship that fitted me be the relationship with Marynia? I had to trust in her to still want me in her life as I did the work. But I didn't trust myself enough and couldn't see how she could accept the stranger that I was becoming, a stranger even to myself. Looking again at Sharp's words, I wondered, '*Could I, would I follow the good advice from Sharp?*'

Moving through the days of intense sun with no rain in sight, I was filled with questions: '*What the hell's the matter with me? Why am I not as happy as I should be? I've got everything I need and want. I have financial security. I have the freedom of movement and speech and I have a good home in a safe country. I have healthy and financially secure children with their own homes and young families. I have it all.*' Yet, I didn't feel as though I had anything. I didn't have any respect for myself or truly understand what was happening to me.

A final nude image found its way onto the blog site at the end of March, less than a week before our departure to return home to Canada. It was an attempt to depict Rodin's *The Thinker*, one of the ways I had imagined myself in the world.

The time in Costa Rica hadn't just been about my inner turmoil. Most of the time we explored volcanoes, rain forests, Mayan sites, and mountain sides filled with exotic birds and animals. We made a ritual of watching the sun set, we made the community our home for three months including building friendships with neighbours. I continually find myself wanting to tell this other story of our life together, but it isn't the story needed for this book.

We made the journey back to Canada, and as with other years, I was soon overwhelmed with allergies and life in general. The loss of a retreat place to bathe in the rays of the sun, mixed in with the return of allergies, stirred the shadows lurking within. Discouraged, I almost considered abandoning the work of self-healing. I needed a retreat into a sacred space, rather than to abandon the process.

It didn't take long before the rounds of visiting family, the return to the golf course with men who were my community friends, and the tasks of maintaining our home filled the hours and days. Whatever it was that had plagued me, retreated with the busyness. It was as if I had entered a winter season, a time of no psychological growth while waiting for spring and rebirth as a changed man.

Waiting in the background, Marynia struggled as well, not knowing how to support me while at the same time wondering when the ordeal would finally end. Our conflicts had left both of us blaming ourselves for triggering the night storms that then left us drained for days. When the storms passed, we would turn to each other, holding tightly onto each other knowing that life without the other was too unbearable.

I was truly worried about losing Marynia as I became more aware of my defects. In my psychological centre, I felt as if I had sold my soul to the devil, so to speak, while a child to stay sane enough to do all that was expected and needed of me. As a child, it was about survival. Somehow now as a man, I had continued to hold onto that early life belief system and life-script.

I had frequently been told I behaved like a child during our spousal conflicts leaving Marynia to feel like the "bad, controlling mother." I hadn't yet made the connection between my triggered responses and the deep underlying causes of a mother-complex that needed to be addressed. It was the mother-complex rather than the father-complex that was now demanding my attention. And, I resisted like some defiant child disobeying his mother. And, as often had happened in the past, what I was reading in Jungian psychology books echoed with what was happening in my outer life.

I turned to a book I had read more than a decade earlier, by James Hollis. I did so because of plans for yet another photo book that would become the fourth book in the Through a Jungian Lens series. And as always, ideas missed in earlier readings leapt out to capture my attention.

> "So a man, during the Middle Passage, has to become a child again, face the fear that power masks, and ask the old questions anew. They are simple questions: "What do I want? What do I feel? What must I do to feel right with myself?" Few modern men allow themselves the luxury of such questions. So they trudge off to work and dream of retiring to play golf on some Elysian Field, hopefully before the heart attack arrives. Unless he can humbly ask these simple questions and allow his heart to speak, he has no chance whatsoever. He is bad company for himself and others."

Those same questions had been asked during the night storms. Typically, I retreated into childlike responses, into triggered knee-jerk responses that should have informed me that I was under the spell of a complex, a mother-complex. In the grips of a complex, there was no rational way I could hear and respond to those basic questions that kept being repeated and repeated each time the night storms raged.

As the summer wore on, I boarded a plane headed to visit my ailing mother. As I flew to visit her and her consort, I had hopes of talking with her about my father and my childhood. I had hoped to get answers that would fill in the gaps of my memories. The real purpose of the visit was to deal with her worsening health issues that were making her independent living increasingly difficult to maintain.

While visiting her, I found myself needing to escape, looking for excuses to walk through the town or to drive to another town rather than sit with her. I knew I should have been spending the hours with her, and the guilt weighed heavily. Yet, I had to escape. I soon became a regular visitor at a coffee house where I could hook into the Internet and write blog posts.

My mother refused to talk about anything from the years growing up as her first-born child. All that she would tell me, and anyone else within hearing distance, was that I was the perfect son, her "golden child."

By the time I left her place, arrangements had been put into place to enable her to move into assisted-living accommodation. It was left to my younger brother, who lived nearby, to help make it happen. My job had been to get her to finally agree to the plans for her care.

Back home in Elrose, the decision was made to return to teaching at the same university in China. Both of us realised that I needed to be teaching rather than sitting at home unoccupied. Teaching gave me purpose in life. The university in Changzhou willingly accepted the application to return. Since there wasn't a lot of time to go through the process of obtaining visas and preparing for the return to China, I made a quick trip to Calgary where I could get the proper visas within a day.

I was glad when the decision to leave home again was made and formalized. All that was left was to make the rounds of visiting, attend weddings, family reunions, and to golf. Together, in the last days before we began the journey back to Changzhou, we prepared the house for a ten-month absence.

Chapter Twenty-One – China Part Two

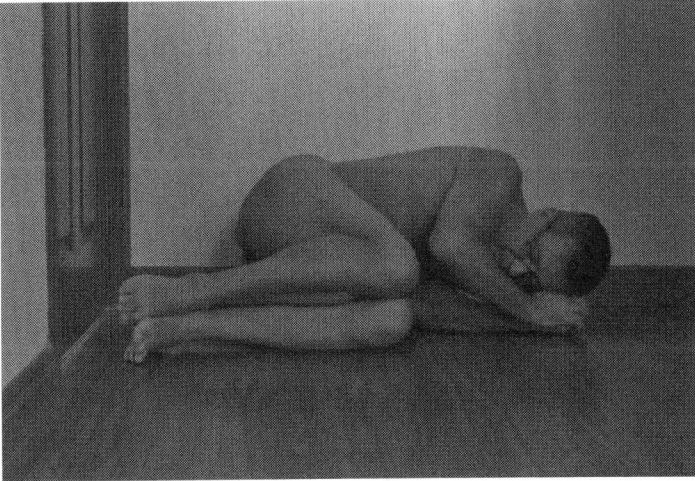

Just wishing it all would end,
caught in darkness and depression, Changzhou 2011.

We flew to Toronto, planning on several days of visiting Dorian and his young family. He had relocated to the city for his career. After several days together, we flew off to the Far East. I had created a new blog site for the return to China.

In a blog entry for September 1, 2010, I wrote:

> "*I lack the courage and the temperament to stick out, to risk being in full view of others. I prefer to keep low and stick to the shadows and not be noticed all that much, at least most of the time. Personally, I prefer to take risks and go out on a limb within my inner landscapes. There I know I have my privacy, safety, and there I have the courage to do what I would never consider doing in the outer world. So, what does that say about me?*"

The evidence left behind over the years in the wake of dealing with psychological issues, told a different story. I had made my pain public in local newspapers, in books, in private conversations, in the world of cyberspace conversations, and in numerous blog posts, including three written earlier the same year that contained nude images of me.

I had been creating a fraudulent image of myself. I was hiding, running away from some very vital truths. Those truths needed to be told, truths of life lived before knowing Marynia. Instead, now at the age of sixty-one, I was once again a VIP in a foreign country. In China I was, the Master Teacher and I reveled in that role, a very public role in a city of four and a half million people.

The city of Changzhou had changed as much as I had changed, in the two years since we had last been there. Despite those changes, I charged into the world of teaching at the university with confidence. And in the role as lead teacher for the expats, I was given the role of mentoring, a role that resonated, as I had once mentored teachers in the schools where I served as a principal. My ego swelled and again hubris blinded me to the small cracks that were showing up in the privacy of our apartment home. What was going on behind the scenes, beneath the control of ego? The answer was buried in a post: *"with a complex activated, the drama unfolds, and life becomes a confused mess."*

The initial energy of being back in China saw my ego validated in so many ways and made the first months of teaching race by. However, like a person suffering from bipolar disease, that initial "high" wore thin and the "lows" were waiting patiently in the wings for their turn to emerge.

Following a visit to Shanghai and the World Expo, the signs of an approaching period of depression began to appear. They showed up in small conflicts. My awareness of this seeped out into a blog post:

> *"When a relationship hits a rocky patch, it pretty much looks like everything is going downhill, down into a dark hole. One's field of vision is reduced to a*

narrow band of possibility, and the possibility is in darkness, a damp darkness that reminds one of swamplands at night, where sinkholes are just waiting to suck one down. In an instinctive reaction we lash out hoping to back off the demons and find a bit of breathing space. The enemy is out there, and the enemy is wearing the body of one's partner in relationship." [October 24, 2010]

Projections were again at work. Triggers were continuing to be activated. I believed those triggers had been deactivated through conscious intentions. Yet, Marynia had again become the victim of my irrational fears. Though I knew Marynia wasn't the enemy, the activated complexes didn't care what I knew; they were determined to get out of their prisons and get their day to speak. I needed to know about who and what I was, and only attention to the complexes would have that happen. With the intention of protecting Marynia, I began to build a wall between myself and her, trying to keep her safe from my demons.

The life of teaching raced along despite the small dramas being acted occasionally in our apartment. Life in China continued to work its wonders during most of the hours of the day. Outside of these sporadic conflicts, we had chosen a four-week tour of Indochina for the term break, with most of that time to be spent in Vietnam. And as was my habit, I buried myself in research of the places to be seen.

-

We flew into Ho Chi Minh City on January 13, 2011 where we began to experience a new culture. I had assumed from research and preparations, that I would see Vietnam through a masculine filter, a land with a long history of war, a country that was filled with temples and other structures that celebrated the masculine. Yet my journal told a different story:

"Water – the unconscious – anima – my soul. Somehow, the feminine has stepped forward to claim my attention. I have taken almost two thousand photos in five days and I would have to say that images of women and water account for most of these images. I do find men in this collection of photos and the temples that men have built, but not all that many. I am often disconcerted as women look into my eyes and smile with invitation while I walk down the streets of the towns and cities while holding Marynia's hand." [January 19, 2011]

The Buddhist temples and the symbols found in so many places, through which we travelled, awoke a desire within me to return to the practice of meditation. In the past I had used meditation as a practice that would help quieten the shadows and ghosts hidden within. But I soon pushed the desire for meditation into the background, telling myself that it wasn't yet time, that I had too few hours in Indochina for meditation.

Two weeks after our arrival in Vietnam, we boarded a plane in Hanoi to fly to Laos, a country that felt like the holiest country either of us had ever been in. The face of Buddha was found in almost every aspect of the country. That sense of holiness which appeared, was mirrored in what was happening within me. I was being pulled into a spiritual place of awe and wonder. Not only darkness lay within me; there was a matching sense of holiness, a pinpoint of golden light for me to follow out of inner darkness.

I took a photo in Luang Prabang, of a young man casting out a net from the shoreline into the Mekong River and wrote in my journal:

"I feel somewhat like this young man, casting my net out into the waters of the unconscious in hopes of netting something that will feed me, and perhaps feed

others. So, I continue this journey of images through Indochina. The images will bring ripples to my psyche and result in moving further down a road I know I am supposed to be travelling." [January 30, 2011]

There were many ripples resonating from the photos I took. I was seeing the world through a different lens. I sensed that it would be in the images where I would later find what I had missed with my senses. The images weren't just about recording the trip, they were more than that. They were evoking hidden truths and would figure into my inner work in the months yet to come.

As we travelled, we met with many faces of poverty. Our hearts broke, especially when those faces of poverty were of children. The children were dirty, usually naked and vulnerable, to whatever brutality that chose them as victims. Seeing them, I saw my own naked vulnerability as a child. The scenes evoked memories of senseless poverty, within which I had grown up, the disconnectedness, the feeling of being lost. Yet, for all the poverty, the nakedness, and the dirt; the children seen in Indochina were still able to play, though surrounded by garbage. I felt guilty for having so much as an adult while these children had as close to nothing as it was possible to get.

From Laos we travelled to Cambodia and the wonders of Angkor Wat, Angkor Thom, and Baryon. The ruins left us speechless and filled with awe. We travelled through floating cities. And always as we travelled, there was the presence of a past that had been so brutal to humans, a past of despots and privileged royalty, which had impoverished the country.

While in Cambodia, in the city of Phnom Penh, I took a photo of a baby sleeping in a dumpster that was filled with trash, with the family seated next to the dumpster. I knew they were street people. The image of the baby sleeping in the dumpster haunted me for days.

Returning to Vietnam, I finally had time for thinking, for decompressing.

> *"The baby sleeping in the trash cart is symbolic of the self, a self that is denied as we buy into the persona, we find ourselves in at birth and the personae we build more luxurious prisons to escape the prisons in which we were born. We come to believe we are the masks we wear, that the shadows we flee from are "others" and not really "our" own shadows. We disown and disinherit the baby in the trash cart. This is how we end up working so hard to drown the denied baby self in all manner of substances and activities. Yet, the baby reappears at night in our dreams, pleading for us to remember self, to reinvest in self. The baby is a symbol of promise and hope, letting us know that all is not lost, that we are not lost."* [February 9, 2011]

I was angry, angry at the world for allowing such poverty. I was angry with myself for being so quiet in the face of what was happening in the outer world. I felt shame and guilt because I had more than I needed. Yet, I was powerless to change the situation. I knew that even if I gave everything to help the poor, the money would only go to feed the voracious hunger of the obscenely rich. I would end up being as destitute as the beggars I would have tried to help. I felt guilty for having escaped the poverty of my own childhood. I was angry, and I needed to step back from it all and breathe, to let time and space dissipate an inner rage.

The journey through Vietnam, Laos, and Cambodia had done a lot to heal the tensions between me and Marynia. Finding myself immersed in countries where Buddhism was at home, something rekindled within me. I had unconsciously abandoned the practice of meditation. And now, I consciously returned to meditation. I began to earn a measure of peace.

That feeling of wellness was picked up by Marynia, encouraging her to hope again. Our time in Indochina was magical, with no night storms to spoil that magic. Still, it was almost with relief that we returned to Changzhou. It wasn't yet time to return to classes, so we were both able to re-establish our bearings in China. As I waited to return to the classroom, I had a lot of time for reflection. Our lesson plans were all in place as were our term plans. I now had time to deal with some of the more than ten thousand photos taken in Indochina.

I returned to writing in my journal to illustrate the questions that pre-occupied me. The words presented in the journal also pointed to what was yet to come though I didn't consciously know what was hidden in those words.

"It's no wonder that I resonate with so much of Jungian psychology. Images are vital to how I interact with the world. The images aren't only those found in my photos, they are also found in music, my words, in my dreams, and in the appearance that I present of myself to the world. Images are also found in the way I speak to others." [February 17, 2011]

Images, they were numinous images, a portal to a different dimension, a fractal dimension exposing a universal, rather than a personal truth. There was no question that the separation between inner and outer worlds was blurring for me. I was beginning to connect to a collective shadow. Earthquakes, tsunamis, wars, politics, the voracious greed of bankers and corporations were eating at the soul of the world, and in turn, they were eating at my soul. The time spent in Indochina had softened my core, making me more sensitive to the world, more vulnerable to the inner shadows.

Then spring came with sunshine and colours to again lift my spirits. The emerging colours of spring banished the ghostly shadows. It was at this time, a visitor from Canada came to stay with us for a week. Life eased back into normal with my full energies returning. I again found myself teaching with an old and familiar passion.

The posts on the blog sites continued to plumb psychological depths. I thought that I was teaching others about Jungian psychology. But in truth, the selection of photos and the reflections that swirled around those Jungian ideas had a different purpose.

> *"I am discovering, uncovering my "self" in a way that is transparent and honest. There is nothing to hide, nor any reason to hide that which I discover, as the bits of shadow exposed enter into my consciousness and cease to be shadow."*

I had unconsciously begun a journey into the inner depths. Time was running out. I was going to have to take some serious time-outs to do the work being demanded by my psyche. But that needed time was deliberately put on hold. We signed contracts to work for another year at the university. I wasn't ready to heed the Call to depth work.

-

Once we had finished giving exams, we returned to Canada during the second week of June, with a stop off in Toronto to again visit Dorian and his family. No sooner had we landed, when my allergies reappeared. It seemed so strange how the allergies retreated into the background while we were in China, Mexico, and Costa Rica, but when back in Canada, they reappeared with a vengeance.

I arranged to have an appointment in Toronto with an allergy specialist in order to try a different approach to solving the problem of allergies. I was tired of being a victim of my body. I loved our home in Canada and there just had to be some way to allow me to enjoy that Canadian home. The status quo had to change. It was time for changes.

Chapter Twenty-Two – Premonitions about Mother

Brothers and the problem of mother, July 2011.

One of the first things I did upon reaching home, was to book return flights to China. Because of the planned vacation of the allergy specialist in Toronto, I needed to return to Toronto earlier. Marynia decided she would fly to Toronto later as she sensed that I could use some time alone without her. She knew that if she was present in Toronto, I would invest most of my energy in her than in myself.

Back home, we returned to a normal. But changes were happening. I had begun to meditate again sitting on cushions so that I could feel the cool air on my bared body. Meditation while nude meant were no body sensations that would distract me from the work of clearing my mind of racing and crazy thoughts.

The feeling of freedom, a freedom to breathe through my pores pulled me to explore even more about nudity. Those experiences showed up on the blog site. I began to speak and write openly about nudity, naturism, sacredness, and authenticity. The words in my posts were about searching for truths about myself than naturism. Somehow the masks of ego and persona behind which I had hidden, began to soften and disintegrate.

It was at this time I remembered moment from the past when Natalie, our middle child asked, *"Papa, what do you really look like?"* She wondered about my face which had been hidden behind a beard I had worn for decades. And so, I asked myself, *'Who am I beneath the beard? Who am I beneath the roles I have lived? Who am I beneath the clothes I wear? Who am I beneath my skin?'* The beard came off, and that question was answered for her and our other two children.

The relationship with my body had been almost non-existent in the past. Despite work, the running on roads and trails, and the occasional skinny-dipping, my primary relationship was with my ego. I almost always was preoccupied with what was in my head. I had defined myself as philosopher and as a psychologist of sorts. I lived and thrived and suffered in my head. I didn't look in the mirror. Even photos were rare.

In contrast, while in nude meditation I began to reconnect with my whole self. Two weeks after our return to Canada, I wrote my first blog post about naturism. That first post lead to three more including this entry in the second post:

"I know that I have found peace in nature, especially when clothing is set aside for a brief time. I have found that peace in lakes and in gentle pools along various rivers, walking through a Yucatan estuary, on protected areas along seashores, in isolated fields and meadows while walking down remote trails in the wilderness. This is not about social activity or about sexual gratification. This is about being honest with oneself, stripping away yet one more mask and

exposing all the flaws so that they can be accepted as natural aspects of self rather than as deficits." [June 25, 2011]

It wasn't long before I was going outside of our home, into abandoned places, empty spaces in the prairie hills, to re-experience being sky clad, stripping off my clothing while outdoors in nature. Marynia was accepting of my naturist activity as she had seen how nude meditation had been calming me. Her only concern was that I made sure that this nudity was kept to places where no one would see me.

However, the addition of naturist posts to the blog site was a different story for her. Too many people we knew read the posts on the blog site. It was one thing to write about naturism in intellectual terms, but when it became personal disclosures, it was no different than stripping off my clothing in public. Whatever others read about my relationship with nudity, impacted upon her.

In response to Marynia's concern, I created a new blog site devoted to naturism. Few people, if any among the people in our lives, would know about the naturist blog site. I made sure that I kept the blog site *safe,* with safe meaning no full-frontal nudity. And, safe also meant keeping the existence of the blog site quiet.

Walking in the hills away from farmhouses and our prairie town, I would decompress. As I walked the hills, I typically had the camera with me. I took many photos of birds, deer, the colours of the land, and the occasional appearance of water during these nude hikes. In the empty spaces of the prairies, I lost my fear of being caught and exposed as a *dirty old man.* Less self-conscious, I seemed to be able to get closer to the wildlife of the prairies. I was very aware of being naked, but I wasn't afraid of it. I was more curious than anything. It didn't take long to wonder what I would see if I took photos of myself in nature.

In the middle of July 2011, we were fortunate to have all of the children and grandchildren gather at the house for a week. As always, their presence was the best present for both of us. When they returned to their own homes, I made another trip to British Columbia to deal with ongoing issues with my mother and her health. She had begun to take dialysis treatments.

My brother and I convinced her to have us appointed as her guardians for health, as well as her power-of-attorneys. We also convinced her to stay in the hospital until a place became available near the hospital. My mother admitted she didn't believe she would ever leave the hospital to live in a nearby hospice.

Hearing my mother talk about her death, I realised this was going to be my last chance to get answers. I again tried to have her tell me the truth about the past. And again, she refused. She denied that there had ever been anything that needed to be said. Knowing that it was going to be the last time I would see her, I left forgiving her as I had forgiven my father more than twenty years earlier. The time for being judgemental was done.

Yet, I returned home very frustrated and angry. There were only a few more weeks left at home in Canada before I had to fly off to Toronto ahead of Marynia. In the days that remained before the flight, those precious days when it was just the two of us, I wrote:

> "In the swamplands of Mexico, I somehow found my footing where nothing was visible from the surface, avoiding sinkholes and hidden dangers. In my dreams, the dream form of my ego, my sense of self seemed to know where to take the next steps forward regardless of the strange and often forbidding landscapes. When confronted with a mountain barrier or an ocean, I simply flew through the mountain or

through the depths of the sea without fear. And in all of these scenes I am naked, unclothed. There are no masks, no costumes, no mirrors to distract or distort. In these scenes, the hidden self, the essential me is seen." [August 11, 2011]

I spent ten days in Toronto before Marynia joined me. With her arrival in Toronto, we celebrated Marynia's birthday and then our anniversary before flying off to China for what would prove to be our last term of teaching in Changzhou.

Chapter Twenty-Three – Mother is Dead and the Mother Complex Lives On

A cave becomes a womb as I grieve my mother's death
in the Philippines, November 2011.

Returning to Changzhou, I was more focused that I had any right to expect. The preparation of documents needed by the university, especially the term plans, as well as getting a good start on the lesson plans that would be needed for classes were less of a challenge than in the past years. I had put in enough time to know what was needed. As we met with the other expat teachers, and the cooperating Chinese teachers, I was given a lot of respect as the oldest instructor at the university with thirty-five years of experience, including my experience at the university. We were off to a great start for the fall term.

I woke from a troubling dream in the early hours, one week after our return to Changzhou. The dream was attempting to warn me that I was entering once again into the swamplands and that there was no turning back, no escaping the work that lay ahead:

"... I walk for what seems to be hours and watch as the background scene changes ... the water beside the road has forced the road to become a narrow, sandy path which presses closer ... I look ahead and see the golden, sandy trail disappearing into the distance ... I know I can't make it to the end of the trail as I will be too hungry and weak ... I sit down thinking I should turn back ... I resist that thought and go on ... the path gets too narrow and I sense I will fall off the path into the water so I get down on all fours and slowly crawl forward ... the trail disappears under the water and I lose sense of direction ... turning to look back, all I see is water ... there is no way to go back and I don't know the way forward ..."
[September 6, 2011]

I was entering a strange place in my head. On the naturist blog site, I had begun to post conversations between my ego and my shadow, with the ego clothed and the shadow stripped bare. The shadow was challenging the ego to be honest, to stop hiding and pretending. The boundaries between ego and the outer world and inner world were slowly dissolving. It seemed only a matter of time before I would find myself lost somewhere between both worlds.

As I continued blogging, I engaged in a process of active imagination. It is as if the brain creates a dream state. During this time, the Jungian Lens blog posts talked of active imagination, while in the Naturist Lens blog posts engaged in using active imagination.

The practice of meditation begun to occur almost daily. Since we had different instruction times, I typically would meditate while Marynia was teaching. I would meditate nude, with gentle music playing in the background. I described, in my journal, the value and need for both blogging and meditation:

"I notice that my blogging is a ritual, a practice I engage in to honour my journey and to light the path on this journey. For me, blogging, is daring to step into ideas and paths that lead me out of my comfort zone of what I know. Blogging as a ritual. It seems to me that the paths of rituals are endless. Silent meditation is one path that I have used and will continue to use though the form of meditation seems to change. Sometimes the meditation is active such as in wandering with the camera. Sometimes the meditation is passive as in sitting still with music or incense or simply with a quiet centre." [September 19, 2011]

I had begun to be more agitated and emotionally unstable when time and circumstance got in the way of both blogging and meditation.

As September 2011 came to an end, I began to find my inner space shifting. Correspondently, there was a shift into a new round of depression and lethargy. That shift had timed itself to match messages and phone calls about my mother. She was giving up on life and was talking about quitting dialysis. Over the next month communications with my brother became more frequent and frantic. I tried to coax my other siblings into visiting our mother before her death. With the spiralling crisis around her eating at my time and thoughts, I began to slip behind in the process of lesson preparation for both myself and Marynia. I turned to recycling old lessons, another page out of the past which had resurfaced.

With the preoccupation with classes and my mother, Marynia and I didn't go for an exploration of a new part of China during the National Holiday. Rather, we spent our time walking around Changzhou, visiting favourite places and taking some needed time to catch up on course documentation and planning. The woman in charge of all foreign teachers had invited us to tour a park with her, her husband, and daughter. This family had become our closest Chinese friends and they wanted to share time together with us while their daughter was home from university classes. As friends, we had eaten in each other's homes, toured together, worked together and often laughed together. But, perhaps the most important part of this friendship was that it prevented us from being alone too much together.

In the journal, a few days after this, I wrote:

> *"I wonder if our relationship is about dysfunction. Our life together is inclusive about almost everything. We are basically seen as inseparable; I have changed in significant ways and she has changed in significant ways. In spite of our enmeshed behaviours visible to the outer world, we are separate beings, at times almost strangers to each other. We have to tread gently when confronting these differences, but often the "treading on egg shells" aggravates old wounds, our open sores."* [October 5, 2011]

Night storms had begun to return, and their intensity was frightening both of us. I was once again punching my head, trying to pound out the fear and anger and the ghosts. Just as the week of holidays came to an end, my mother married her consort of thirty-three years. They got married in the hospital between dialysis treatments. My response was one of relief and of anger that it had taken them so long to make their union official. I was angry because it had been my mother who had refused to be married all those years. She needed to believe in her independence.

Days after their wedding, while walking through a park, I saw a young mother with her son who appeared to be about ten years of age, a scene which I captured in a photograph, and wrote about on the Jungian Lens blog site:

> *"I have been thinking of my own mother of late because of serious issues surrounding her health. My*

mother is 79. I don't really want to tell a tale of my mother in my own life as the tale would not really be adequate. There are too many little stories, scenes, poses and vignettes which would need to be presented and then there would still be huge holes in the tale. The mother I experienced, and the mother experienced by each of my brothers and sisters is not the same. We each have left our childhood years with different images and associations with the word mother." [October 18, 2011]

I then began to take a series of on-line courses on Jungian psychology. I was once again running away from something lurking beneath the surface. I had irrationally hoped that by focusing on these new courses while teaching and blogging and meditation, the hungry ghosts bubbling beneath the surface would retreat into the depths where they belonged. And then I bought a guitar and began to play it hoping that music would help keep the demons at bay, as it had in my youth.

A decision was made by Marynia to take a break from teaching, a needed break from the routines of life in Changzhou. Marynia suggested spending a week in the Philippines for sunshine, warmth, and snorkelling. A rearrangement of our classes was approved by the university. Now in our fourth year at the university, we had earned a lot of trust. We both needed to lay back in sunshine, to snorkel, and to enjoy a week of warmth.

Waiting. It had seemed that the time for travelling to the Philippines would never come. I felt stuck, very stuck. In the journal I wrote:

"Sometimes each day begins to morph into other days, almost featureless and not worth remembering. I seem to want more than "waiting" for something as time slips away. Since we all have a limited number

of days and hours to live, I wonder at the pointlessness of some of these days and hours. At times like these, even reading or listening to anything that has depth is avoided as much as possible. I find myself engaged in mindlessness, activities such as playing solitaire against a computer. And noticing my "wasting" of time I get angry with myself, telling myself that I should know better." [November 2, 2011]

Finally, the time to leave for Moalboal on Cebu Island, in the Philippines arrived. We had stretched vacation time to include two weekends, for a break of nine days. The blog post from Moalboal, the next day was pregnant with dark premonitions of what was waiting for us in the Philippines:

"I am sitting on my balcony in a little beach resort in Moalboal, Philippines. I had visions of an isolated set of cottages along a mostly deserted beach, an expectation that faded quickly with the first look at the site and then taking a short walk along the beach. I was both disappointed and angry. Yet, in a way, I was almost expecting to be let down. I spent the night before flying out in Shanghai at the airport hotel with my room number being 6661. My first response was of shock – 666 was the sign of the devil. I immediately took that to mean that my unconscious was about to burst out of its container and make life miserable for me, leaving a trail of wreckage which I would then have to clean up." [November 12, 2011]

Despite that initial feeling, the beach, the villa, and the sea were a beautiful and welcome change from the damp cold in Changzhou that had chilled both of us through to our bones. It didn't take long before I was out taking photos with Marynia, discovering the shorelines, the nearby roads, the sea, and sunsets. We sat back and relaxed and breathed deeply, and finally smiled at each other, happy to be in such a beautiful, warm place together.

-

Two days after arriving in the Philippines, on November 14, 2011, my mother died. Several days later, I was finally able to write:

> "*I have to admit that I haven't been doing as well as I thought since the day my mother died. I had thought that I was prepared for her death knowing that it was coming and having had a week-long visit with her to say our good-byes. It took four days for the tears to finally come and allow the pressure to ease up.*
>
> *I descended into a darkness. I felt an intense guilt about still being alive even though it seemed a part of me had died; it was almost as if the creative inner force within me, my very soul had died. I wanted to disappear, forever, into that darkness. I was forgetting to breathe. A vise had seized my lower stomach and was squeezing for all it was worth and all I wanted was for it to stop, for stop to the pressure and pain.*" [November 17, 2011]

I took refuge in meditation. I meditated in the morning on the upper deck, and again later in the day at a secluded location along the beach. What had been planned as a holiday had become a time for grieving. As the eldest of her children, I tried to communicate to all my brothers and sisters, and all my mother's surviving family to let them all know. I then set up an on-line memorial page so that the extended family spread across most of Canada could meet on-line to share their stories of her. And, in quiet moments I cried. Through all of this, Marynia was my strength, my reason to keep breathing.

Descending into despair over the next few days, it seemed that there were only two things that kept me afloat. One of the two reasons was a retreat into naturism as I had done following the sexual abuse by my maternal grandfather more than forty years earlier. I needed to have control. With no control over my mind and feelings, all that was left was control of my body. However, the primary reason that kept me sane was Marynia. She didn't criticize the increased time for nakedness; rather, she validated it by taking photos of my nude meditations in nature. She pulled me forward to explore the edges of the sea and the edges of civilisation in the surrounding areas. She sat with me, as I mourned. And then, the days used up, we returned to Changzhou and the life of teaching in China.

Back in China, I found questions hounding me for answers, with the darkness pressing in. It seemed, somehow, as if there was something much larger and darker that the death of my mother, and the natural mourning. I avoided that darkness as I kept it at a distance as much as possible. I focused on what I did best. Teaching.

The lessons went well, almost inspired lessons. I set aside expectations of what "should" be done, for what was more enlivening for the students. Their efforts and responses affirmed within me that I was a master at this craft of teaching. However, what I gave to them I couldn't give to myself or to Marynia.

November slipped into December and life became quieter and less busy with the classes missed finally made up. The annual round of Christmas activities had yet to begin. I began to read a new book that I had carried with me to China, based on Marynia's recommendation. She had read it, a book called Fire and Irises. In the pages of Nicol's book I heard so many echoes.

"From the outside I suppose I looked as though I was fairly 'together.' I was a psychologist and held a full-time job, which I did adequately. But that was the cover story. I despaired that I would never be normal and wake up feeling happy like other people."

As I stared at these words, I realised that these words could have been written by me. It didn't take long to read the book.

Because of the guitar I was conscripted to perform at the university's Christmas concert. I was also cast in the role of Santa Claus, with the task of giving out the treats to the students who gathered in the auditorium that seated a good portion of the campus. When it was my turn to perform, I sang, "The Angels Cried." I couldn't find it within myself to sing some cheery song about Christmas, or snowmen, or wonderlands of snow.

On Christmas Day, 2011, a sunny and warm day, Marynia and I had taken a walk to the Metro store to buy some "foreigner" food, and to stock up on Chilean wine. We had company coming for an evening meal at our place. With the groceries bought and the backpacks filled, we began the half-hour walk back to the apartment. I had only managed to make it to the edge of the parking lot when I suddenly stopped and sat down in a state of shock.

I was being assaulted by image after image from the past, images of sexual involvement with my mother. The woman whom I had honoured only a month earlier, had been a sexual predator. Scenes of myself at the age of ten were the first to emerge with what seemed like a deliberate attempt to have me return to her womb, images of a little boy suffocating with his face pressed into her womb. I was terrified. *'Is this real? Am I making it up?'*

It was the beginning of a flood of ongoing nightmares and flashbacks which would wake me in the middle of the night, screaming and lashing out with fists to protect myself from the monsters hiding in the nightmares.

As the end of term approached, before our departure for a term break holiday in Thailand, I was once again scrambling for marks and documentation. The same scene had marked my breakdown in 1998. I was sinking and sinking too fast. We both hoped that holiday time in the warmth and sunshine of Thailand would allow me to regain some stability. We both already knew that this was going to be our last year in China.

-

We arrived in Thailand on January 9, 2012. The warmth and the late afternoon sun felt like heaven after the damp, penetrating cold of Changzhou. The condo was large enough to give Marynia and me a sense of space with its European elegance. I believed that this was just what I needed. I continued to meditate, finding the perfect location on a small balcony where I could soak in the sunshine while nude.

Both of us took the time to go for long walks to explore the community of Pattaya. In the other hours of the day, when we weren't walking, I returned to writing. I needed to record the images that had continued to emerge, to have them become part of my story. I took occasional breaks, so we could spend time together at the swimming pool. Gradually, I began to breathe easier; life was once again settling down.

However, new flashbacks began to appear. The intensity of those scenes was reflected again in nightmares. I tackled the nightmares as my own therapist using self-psychology. I didn't retreat from the process of self-analysis. I was tired of being a victim, of not having any control. Besides, I had a significant background in psychotherapy which would assist me in the process. I just needed to keep one part of myself objectively separate as an observer on the sidelines, ready to intervene when the going got too rough or appeared to be getting out of control. The flashbacks and nightmares continued to assault me without regard for my skills and abilities as a mental-health counsellor.

In desperation, finally realising that I couldn't do this all on my own, I sent an e-mail to Zeljko in Canada asking him to consider taking me on as an analysand. I had gone too deep, had become too enmeshed in the shadows in the attempts at self-analysis. I had lost control over the process from the sidelines. I told Marynia that I needed to return to Jungian analysis in Calgary rather than returning to Changzhou to finish off the last term. Marynia was torn between keeping her word, her contract, and of following me back to Canada. Her first response was to honour her contract thinking that I would respond as I had always responded, by accepting her choice and thus postponing my return to analysis until the end of the school year.

Yet, rather than giving in, I held firm and told her that I would go to Canada alone while she finished off her contract. We would be together again in the summer when she returned to Canada. With my decision made, Marynia sent in both resignations to the university. My decision rang true in her ears, and she agreed to go back home to Canada with me. We then began an on-line search for a place to live in Calgary.

I continued to be my own analyst while waiting for our stay in Thailand to come to an end. I continued to wander through the depths and the shadows. The decision to go into analysis gave me renewed courage and hope. My journal records the process:

"The process has me risking self-analysis, taking myself on as a patient, watching the process from the sidelines and recording data and then daring to ask my 'self' some tough questions about what my 'self' has said and seen. If this sounds a bit like

'dissociation, it is. Dissociation is at work, but it has always been at work to some extent for as long as I can remember, probably all the way back to my early childhood." [January 25, 2012]

Then, the journal went quiet. Together we walked, read, took a few photos of people and places. The last weeks in Pattaya, Thailand were quieter and gentler between the two of us. Marynia followed as I wandered with camera in hand through the edges of community, discovering several Buddhist temples to explore. Buddhism was again showing me a psychological face that had begun to fit with what I understood about being human. I was trying to understand about why I always felt alone, even when surrounded by people who loved and respected me.

The return to Changzhou was not easy for either of us. How could we explain to friends and colleagues that we were leaving a job half done? The simplest answer seemed to be a blend of the truth with some poetic license. I had a cancer of the brain. People understood cancer and accepted it as a sad reality. As we packed during those last five days in Changzhou, I took to slipping into positive memories from the past, memories of the first years spent with Marynia. There was no energy left within me for self-analysis. I needed to retreat into safer inner spaces while waiting to make the transition back, into the safety net of psychoanalysis.

Chapter Twenty-Four – Jungian Analysis in Calgary Part Two

A mandala born out of analysis – the complexity of self-definition, spring 2012.

"I realise that even though I am home in Canada, I am 'un étranger.' We are all strangers, even within our own families and communities, even if we have never left our home communities. In truth, we are mostly strangers to ourselves." [February 16, 2012]

We stopped in Toronto to spend a few days with Dorian and his family before flying home to Saskatchewan. The few days in Toronto renewed my belief in family as I saw the young family actively engaged in their new life, in a new home. In this setting, I looked at Marynia and knew why she had sacrificed and endured so much in our relationship. It all about love. She had been on this journey before in 1998. She had given up a home and career to go where I needed to go, once that process of analysis was done. Again, she had given up another career she loved because it was what I needed. But what did she need? I could only guess that what she needed was to be with me, to help me get well. She had invested more than forty years in our marriage, and she wasn't going to quit. I saw all that in Toronto and wrote in the Jungian Lens blog site:

> "*Like me, she has to hold the tension, waiting and hoping that this time the process will do what it needs to do in order to allow her to have her life back. And it is there that I finally understand something important. Her life, similar to my life, is one that is only whole in relationship. The loss of relationship would be the greatest loss. Embracing relationship as whole individuals, even as broken individuals, is what animates us.*" [February 19, 2012]

On February 24th, I had my first session with Zeljko. I woke up that morning, before dawn, to sit still in the living room of the basement suite we had rented in Calgary. I took a photo of the dawn. The sky appeared to be on fire, red fire. I thought of the old expression, "Red sky in the morning, sailors take warning." And that had me worry more about what I was unleashing by this move back into Jungian analysis. I was terrified about screwing it all up this time, and that the analyst was going to refuse to work with me. '*Will I be able to give the right answers to Zeljko's questions?*' was a question that gnawed. I worried that I would become too silent and hide behind meaningless words because I was ashamed.

Zeljko already knew quite a bit about me, but he set all that aside and focused on doing the foundational work of building a safe place for the analytical work to happen. Without that foundation, the analytic process would fail. The journey of healing had begun again, the journey which had begun fourteen years earlier in the same city.

As the first weeks passed, I struggled even though Marynia was beside me all the moments when I wasn't in analysis. It got harder and harder to navigate the hours in between sessions. I tried desperately to be a deserving partner for her, to share some sort of a normal life and do some normal things with her. She deserved at least that much. I felt guilty for not being present enough, though I was physically beside her. My nightmares woke her, and we would then lay beside each other worried.

Reaching back into the past in search of answers, I remembered needing to devote a lot more of the healing time in solitary silence. In addition to solitude, I needed to meditate, to draw, to write, and to play music. A new guitar was purchased as the old one too damaged to play anymore. I left the guitar I bought in China in Changzhou. I had hoped that music would be yet another tool to aid in the journey of healing.

I also began to attend Buddhist meditation evenings. I wanted to learn more about Buddhism and build a better foundation for meditation practice. Each week took me deeper into the mysteries of Tibetan Buddhism, which seemed to help me navigate the days that slowly made their way towards spring.

Two months into analysis, I asked Marynia to return home in Elrose, to leave me in Calgary, and to trust in me to work through the process. I would make the journey back home every second weekend, as I had done fourteen years earlier. I knew he needed the space in which to fall apart without having to see the pain that my falling apart caused in her. I needed to not worry about failing to be present enough with her.

I sent her home and felt like a traitor to our marriage because of it. She had given up her teaching and followed me, and now it was as if I was rejecting her. I didn't know how to explain that I wasn't rejecting her; I was trying to stop rejecting myself, stop denying myself the full attention needed for healing.

A storm erupted with this decision. Like so many storms in the past, I turned on myself destructively. I deleted the naturist blog site, deleted my journal, and deleted photos of me from the photo archives. I wanted to erase myself, and I wanted it all to end. And, as so often in the past, I struck out at her by punching myself in the head. Yet, it wasn't her I was trying to punish, it was my mother, the woman who had raped me. I was punishing myself for allowing my mother, and so many others in the past, to sexually abuse me.

I didn't see myself as a man who deserved to have a wife. I believed the criticisms of not having the balls to stand up for myself. Yet this was exactly what I had just done, I had finally stood up for myself. Yet, for all of that, I would have backed down if Marynia would have pressed me.

-

At the beginning of May, I found a smaller and less expensive basement suite, in a different location, one that was closer to the analyst's office. With that move, I was officially on my own, very alone. I took refuge in Buddhism, played the new guitar, wrote down night dreams, wrote blog posts, walked and walked, took an occasional photograph, and waited to see where Jungian analysis was taking me.

I had placed all bets on analysis and meditation practice. However, in the process, I forgot about taking care of my body. The stresses of analysis weren't being countered by any conscious attention to eating habits or exercise. I ignored the need for proper rest. As a result, my weight soared along with my blood pressure.

A doctor confirmed the high blood pressure and I was placed on medications. I was shocked by and began to walk instead of driving everywhere. My diet changed as well. I walked for hours at a time focusing on pace and distance, as I once had done when training for marathons. My new goal was to simply find a way to get well in body, mind and spirit.

"It's been almost three months since I have returned to analysis, to the work of diving deep into the darkness of an inner world in order to reconnect and remember. Now, there seems to be a sense that a light is beginning to rekindle my external life with a new sense of energy and urgency, an upwelling of libido which demands that I live fully in my body as well as in my head. Yes, there is an urgency in this as the years of my life are racing towards a return to the source of all being. I am being told, 'don't sit back and wait for a better time, for this is the time, now!'
[May 20, 2012]

As analysis progressed in Calgary, I would go home to Marynia every second week-end. As in the past, the journey between Calgary and home was difficult, especially the return trip back to Calgary.

Time apart for analysis wasn't working as well as it had in the past. There was a brooding sense that I would have to make a choice between a new life that included on-going analysis with the likelihood of becoming an analyst; or a returning home with the risks of again breaking down and causing all sorts of suffering for Marynia and others. This fear often became a focus of the analytical sessions which seemed to point me towards remaining in the Calgary area.

Zeljko encouraged my dream of becoming a Jungian analyst that dated back to a time before my first round of Jungian analysis. Mae, the other Calgary analyst, echoed the idea when we met again at a Jungian event in the city. I was stuck between these opposing poles, as it basically came down to choosing a life with or without Marynia.

Each week I would visit the Marpa Gompa Buddhist centre for Buddhist meditation. I would go early to the centre and walk around the area before the meditation sessions. Near the end of May 2012, I began to read a new book by Chögyam Trungpa called, Smile at Fear.

> "We also have to give up the notion of a divine savior, which has nothing to do with what religion we belong to, but refers to the idea of someone or something who will save us without our having to go through any pain ... If you are really interested in working with yourself, you can't lead that kind of double life, adopting ideas, techniques, and concepts of all kinds simply in order to get away from yourself ... Nobody can save you from yourself."

I heard the same words that had already been said many times by Marynia, by Zeljko, and by others I had met along the way. I was finally ready to really hear these words. I had to own my physical health and mental health.

The shift to include the body, was matched by a new quest, to walk the Camino de Santiago. I had envisioned making the walk, a three-month long journey leaving from either Paris or Le Puy en Velay. After doing a lot of research from a variety of online sources, I decided that Le Puy would be the starting point. With the vow made to walk the Camino, I realised that this would require a break in analysis.

For a while, I kept this vow, not mentioning it to either Marynia or Zeljko. Before I could let anyone know, I needed to see if my body would be strong enough for the pilgrimage. My body responded well as I walked to and from analysis when the weather was cooperative, a round trip that was about fourteen kilometres long. I then bought new shoes and a few other hiking essentials for the Camino.

In June, I took two weeks off from analysis while Zeljko went for a holiday in Europe. I returned home for those two weeks. I meditated and did some golfing with Marynia and friends. We spent quality quiet time together. For those two weeks life once again felt almost normal.

It wasn't long after returning to Calgary when I watched a movie called 'The Way.' I sent a message to Marynia to have her watch the movie as well. The movie had reinforced my intention to walk the Camino. I now felt brave enough to let both Marynia and Zeljko know about my intention to walk the Camino. Zeljko was confused as to why I would do this, especially since there was a lot of work still to do together. Marynia simply stayed quiet.

Analysis continued as if the intention to walk the Camino had never been mentioned. Zeljko had encouragement me to return to university for a Master of Counselling Psychology degree which would then be the launching pad to begin analytical training at a Jungian institute.

I said little in response and then said even less about my Camino plans. It began to feel as if his analysis was becoming all about the analyst. It wasn't, but I couldn't see it any other way at the time. I responded with a quiet decision to take a fork in the road, away from being a Jungian analyst. Every trip back home taught me that my real life was at home with Marynia. That was my future.

Part Four

A Pilgrimage of Healing

"The particular reasons which drive an individual towards an act of pilgrimage are inevitably deeply personal, and in many cases beyond the exercise of logic alone. Even though the physical dangers are not as great as they once were, the psychological and spiritual ferment remains. Those who are close to the pilgrim may well ask why they have undertaken such an action. The act of pilgrimage disturbs the lives of those who surround the pilgrim."

Nicholas Shrady – Sacred Roads

Once out of the protected container of analysis, the real journey of healing finally begins. To fall or to remain standing is a moment by moment adventure.

Chapter Twenty-Five – Pilgrim

The Cathedral in Conques
a place where ghosts were released, September 2012.

In late June, while sitting and reading on the back deck at home, feeling *at home*, I arrived at a decision with regards to continuing analysis.

"Marynia, I'm not going back to analysis in Calgary."

"Why?" she asked with some alarm.

"If I go back to analysis, it will only end up bad. Zeljko has counselled me that I need to set out on my own. If I understood him correctly, all that will do is to take me away from you."

"Maybe he is right," Marynia offered. "Maybe you need to be free to become better."

"I can't have a future without you in it. Zeljko isn't right. You do more for me and my mental health than I could ever do on my own. Not only am I not returning to analysis, I'll be going to walk the Camino. It is something that I have to do for me, to finally put the ghosts to rest."

Marynia was filled with doubts. Maybe Zeljko was right. Maybe she was getting in the way of my healing. They were so different in so many ways. She had often told me that I should find someone else so that I could truly be happy. She didn't want me out of her life, but she didn't want me to keep suffering either. Despite what I had said, she began to wonder if he would leave her. She had as many self-doubts in our relationship as I did.

I returned to Calgary in the first week of July for a last set of analytical sessions. The shift which had happened within me, was now taking me on a pilgrimage in search of healing and forgiveness. I needed to feel it in my body, this forgiveness of myself and all of those who had abused me in the past.

During those final two weeks in Calgary, I hiked with determination, as if possessed to push to the point of exhaustion. Analysis became just something I did in the background when I wasn't walking, reading, writing, doing meditation, and simply being alone with myself. Though I hadn't taken the first step on the Camino path, I had already become a pilgrim.

As I read a book about being a pilgrim, I realised that disturbing the lives of others was something I hadn't thought of very much. My intention was to disturb and banish the ghosts of the past so that they would leave me alone.

Although, though the pilgrimage was still a month and a half away, I could feel my body respond to the deliberate stresses of training. Meditation practice became deeper in response, my ego had become stronger. I was finding the necessary will power to break out of dependence on others and the dependence on analysis. This was the whole point, the goal of going into analysis in the first place; to learn how to stand on my own two feet and be a better person with others.

During the last weekend in Calgary, I went into the nearby mountains by Canmore, to challenge myself with physical ascents and descents. I climbed a path I had never been able to climb in the past, because of my fear of heights. I had to confront that fear. I walked on the edge of an abyss as I climbed the path. It reminded me of stories I had read as a youth, stories from the Lives of the Saints where those on their spiritual quests often punished themselves, pushed their limits in search of meaning and connection with their chosen God. Like me, these ancients had searched for something to fill the holes in their hearts and minds. They were pilgrims of a different sort on their own journeys of healing, a journey that I had triggered when I stopped teaching in China.

I left Calgary. Rather than write as I had done for so long, I chose to spend time with Marynia, who now was suffering in advance of my departure. We golfed together, sat still together, cried together, and worried at what the future had in store for us as a couple. At the end of July, I told our adult children and their spouses about my Camino plans. Having disclosed the plans, I then wrote in my journal:

> "*So why am I doing this? Well, it is what I consider to be the next, and hopefully second last part of my healing process. The last part of the process is coming home and staying there with Marynia without being tortured by the demons of my childhood past. This walk is taking place so that I can "walk the Devil out of me." I have, like all people, hurt and scarred people as I moved through life, including in various ways, each of you. And like almost all people, I didn't even know I was leaving a trail of hurt behind me. We hurt each other, and we hurt ourselves despite our best intentions.*
>
> *So, the journey is one of seeking absolution, a forgiveness of my "transgressions," as well as a forgiveness for those who "transgressed against" me.*

That is a very "Catholic" belief. As you know, I have also included Buddhism into my belief system, something that I am finding more and more vital to my sanity. It is teaching me about being at peace with myself. So, as well as praying on this journey, I will take time to meditate.

Between the two, I will, repeat - will - find the inner peace that has been missing for so long. That is the gift I will be bringing home - being at peace with myself so that both your mother and I can enjoy the last twenty to thirty years of our life together." [August 6, 2012]

Everyone came home in August. I explained to them what I was going to do and what the pilgrimage meant. With that said, almost everyone in the family simply accepted it as another step in their Papa's journey of healing. I also talked to them about going silent for the most part while I would be in Europe. I then took a photo of the whole family, which I would carry with me on the Camino. I hoped the photo would ground me, remind me of why I was walking. When everyone had returned home, Dorian wrote to me, a small note that focused on the goal of the pilgrimage:

"The upcoming silence will be the power that heals you. Keep an eye on the 'prize' and know we all love you and support you on this journey." [August 13, 2012]

As the last days passed by, at a lazy summer pace, I worried about the future fallout from the pilgrimage. The words of Nicholas Shrady came back and troubled me: *"The act of pilgrimage disturbs the lives of those who surround the pilgrim."* I might be doing all the walking, but everyone else in my life was going to be affected, disturbed by that very decision to walk. The ripples would flow out to reach everyone in my life. Each, in their own way, would be taking a parallel journey that rippled out from my Camino. I wouldn't be alone, I had never been alone. All of them would be there within me, and that made the decision to get on the plane and leave for Paris just that much easier.

-

I left a letter for Marynia to read on the pillow just before we drove to the airport in Saskatoon. I knew she would read it, and hopefully she would be kind to herself and have a bit more faith in me returning to her a better man than when I had left her.

> *"I am tired of running. I am worn out from running. I am tired of darkness and fear. It seems I can't run far enough or fast enough to get away from me. The act of going on a pilgrimage is not about running away. It puts me into a place, space and time where I am forced with each step, each kilometre and each scene, to be face-to-face with myself. It is about forcing myself to face the facts of who I am without being able to turn to you or our children or our grandchildren as a way to escape facing myself. I have to accept that it is hopeless for you or our children and grandchildren to fill the black holes, or to build a thick enough barrier to permanently bury them – hopeless. I need to be able to turn to myself, to make friends with myself, to trust myself. I know I can't do this at home as the moment I look up and see you, I am undone, falling into the cocoon of you. I see you, my magical other, and avoid looking at me.*

> *Going on this pilgrimage is about love in a big way. If I return able to be my own friend, trusting myself; I will be able to love you more as an equal. You are not my mother and I need to stop giving you a mother's authority over me. It's not about what you do or what you have done; it is about what I do and what I have*

done or not done. So, I go on this pilgrimage walking slowly, one step and one day at a time, to become friends with myself. This is not about running or escaping. I go so that when I return, you will find that your husband is a man, not a child trapped in a man's body. I go so that I can stop being afraid of both living and dying.

I want the next thirty or more years, to be years where we can laugh, play, travel, drink coffee, walk, golf, as equal partners in love and life." [August 19, 2012]

-

The plane to Paris left on time. Arriving in Paris the next morning, I soon made my way to the hostel in Montmartre, located just a few blocks from the Basilique Sacre-Coeur. I had planned on using the time until I left for Le Puy, in retracing the steps of pilgrims from the past who had made their pilgrimages to Santiago, Spain.

Walking in the hot August afternoon from the Basilique Sacre-Coeur to the Tour Saint Jacques, was the first stage of this mini pilgrimage. From there I walked on to the Cathedral Notre Dame where I got his pilgrim's passport stamped.

This hadn't been my first time in the Cathedral, but regardless, the grandeur of the space pulled me to sit for a while. Sitting in a pew in silence, with tears tracing lines down my cheeks, it dawned on me that there was no turning back anymore. This journey of healing had taken me down a path from which there was no turning back. Wiping my eyes, I finally rose and walked out the door.

The Rue Saint Jacques took me to another church, Saint Jacques du Haut Pas, the last planned stop before returning to the hostel. In the late afternoon, I was hot, tired, and had blisters. Inside the church, all the certainties I had built regarding the Camino vanished. I was already falling apart at the seams. I was now adrift. My carefully constructed plans seemed to be falling apart.

That feeling followed me through the rest of the day and into the next morning when I found myself sitting in the wrong train at the station. I hadn't paid enough attention to realise that it was the train which had arrived from Lyon, not the train going to Lyon. When the departure time came and went without the train being boarded by other passengers and leaving the terminal, I finally realised my error. I rushed back to the ticket office to see what could be done to get to Le Puy en Velay that day.

Waking up to the realisation that I needed to be more present, I regained enough focus to deal with the situation. There was no extra cost for new train tickets, except the cost to my pride. Though missed the first train, I wouldn't be late for the pilgrimage registration that afternoon in Le Puy. Because of preparations made while in Canada, I already had a bed booked for the night in Le Puy. The journey to Le Puy went without further mishap. I navigated the change of trains in Lyon and arrived in Le Puy in plenty of time to register for the Camino. The journey had already begun to teach me lessons that needed to be learned.

At the Pilgrim Mass the next morning, I stood with about seventy other pilgrims to get the bishop's blessing, a gift of a rosary and amulet. With the gifts in hand, I went with the others to get my pilgrim passport stamped. Then I left the Cathedral to begin my pilgrimage. I walked longer than planned that first day. The intended stop in Montbonnet was reached, yet I needed to keep moving. I hadn't made any reservations at the hostel in Montbonnet, so I continued to walk on to Saint Privat d'Allier. I met another pilgrim just as I was leaving Montbonnet who had also decided to walk a longer. Together we walked the last few kilometres in silence.

At the private hostel where we stopped for the night, I was reluctant to join in the conversations of others who had walked from Le Puy. I withdrew into my head only to imagine that they were talking about me in negative terms. The long day's hike had left everyone of us exhausted, too tired to be sociable. I couldn't see that.

When most of the other pilgrims had left to go to a local mass, or to wander around the small town perched on the hillside, I turned to meditation with the hopes of escaping a growing sense of paranoia. At the evening meal, the paranoia was gone. I was finally able to interact with the other pilgrims and the owners of the private home, which served the needs of pilgrims.

I continued to walk further than originally planned the second day. I stopped at intervals to sit alongside the path and read from Pema Chodron's book, When Things Fall Apart, or to chart the stops along his journey in the Miam Miam Dodo guide book, which had been purchased in Paris. I walked with a determined purpose; I walked alone. The blisters that had first appeared in Paris, became larger, and walking became more and more difficult and painful. I embraced the pain as penance, almost proud of having to suffer physically.

"As I got ready to start the fourth day of walking, I noticed that I was approaching the coming day's walk with more confidence. If I had been at home, I would have been checking with others to verify my choices, never really trusting myself to make the right choices. On the trail I was forced to make my own choices without turning to anyone else, for there was no one else around, most times not even another pilgrim hobbling down the trail. I walked with more confidence. Even the pain in my feet was helping me. I was learning to cope better with adversity, learning that the adversity was due to my choices, poor

choices. I was learning to dig deeper into my willpower to keep going in spite of the pain, in spite of discouragement." [September 4, 2012]

Leaving Saugues the third morning, I got lost in the pre-dawn light, and had to backtrack into town and search for signs of the Camino trail. I was again reminded to get out of my head and be present, or I was going to continue to get lost. I was learning just what it was that the Camino was supposed to be teaching; at least one of the lessons that needed to be learned.

I still had ghosts and shadows to deal with at some point during the Camino. '*I should have stayed to care for my brothers and sisters rather than leave them at the mercy of my parents,*' was one of many guilty thoughts. I felt guilty for so many things I had done and for those things that had been done to me.

The next day began with fog, and the pilgrims in front of me became like the ghosts in my head. The silence of the fog pressed, as I walked across the eerie landscape of the Aubrac. The way appeared to be littered with large broken rocks, randomly thrown. I came across a crude, wooden shelter shrouded in fog. I entered the shelter and found another pilgrim huddled within it. The two of us talked together, as we had seen each other earlier. The younger man wondered if I was a Buddhist as he had seen me meditating in a hostel as well as along the side of the trail. He was a young German university student named Luca. I listened to his story and we became pilgrim friends.

The rest of the day's walk was done in a better mood, which was matched with the fog lifting. Luca and I found ourselves sharing the same hostel though we had arrived there at different times. We shared a communal meal with a few other pilgrims in the hostel. Then, I went wandering through the village and found the church.

"When I got to the town's cathedral, I soon found myself sitting along one of the sides, in the shadows, where again tears began to fall. Again, I was ready to just quit the whole thing. But even thinking of quitting didn't help stem the tears as then I began to cry at the prospect of returning home and still being lost in my inner darkness. I knew that this was my last hope if I was to emerge sane, to emerge as a man who would be fit to be a husband, father, and grandfather. Finally, I settled back into accepting that I would continue the pilgrimage and risk everything on a positive result. I knew I wasn't there yet, I wasn't ready yet." [September 6, 2012]

I had come so close to quitting, believing that I wasn't good enough to be a pilgrim. The following day was more encouraging as I walked to Espalion. And then, surprisingly, I felt a return of balance, remembering why I was walking the Camino. It was to experience and to exorcise the pain and the ghosts. This was my quest for healing so that I could be a better person. I was walking to save my sanity and my soul. And so, I hurried my steps, anxious to get there faster.

The walk to Conques was marked with this need to hurry. I had a premonition that something important waited for me in Conques, something momentous. I arrived and was immediately disappointed with the Cathedral. The only thing I could then think of was the pain in my feet as I struggled on the cobble stone streets and climbing the steep hills within the tiny town. I knew that it wasn't the Cathedral that seemed to be missing its grandeur, but rather my expectations that had been growing during the day's walk. I let go of my expectations after time for meditation. Then I went out and took a few photos of the town. Back at the municipal hostel I showered, meditated again, and then napped.

I woke from a short, fitful sleep upon hearing other pilgrims enter the hostel dorm to claim their bunks. Quite a few of the original pilgrims who were with me in Saint Privat d'Alliers, as well as a few others I had met further along the Camino, arrived. The group had intended to go back to the Cathedral later in the evening for a presentation by the local priest. After being asked to accompany them, I agreed to become part of their group.

As darkness filled the evening sky, and with a simple meal finished, I went to the Cathedral courtyard to meet with my pilgrim friends. For two of them, this was to be the end of their journey. For most of the others, the journey would last another two days, ending in Figeac. I was the only one in the group who had the intention of walking all the way to Santiago, Spain.

As the scene unfolded during the presentation in front of the Cathedral, I was cast into the role of protector by the women in the group. The other pilgrims had gathered around a woman who felt threatened by a man who was staring intently at her. I took on the role of protector without thinking. The man, who appeared to be a predator, withdrew from proximity to the group when he saw my face and eyes giving him a warning to stay away from the group. Finally, as the evening ended with music in the Cathedral, everyone withdrew from the church leaving me alone in it. Tears began to fall. I was grieving the loss of my innocence as a child. I was angry at the predators in the church who had taken advantage of me as a young boy. And then, when the tears stopped flowing, I left the church and returned to the hostel.

"Once in my bunk, I decided to take some time to meditate. Curiously, sitting in my meditation with a focus on breathing, I began to loosen the tension in my body. I felt a sense of release from the darkness, as though the ghosts that had been in pursuit had finally given up the chase. And then, I slept."

The next day was again filled with the need to hurry forward. The blisters were getting larger. I hurried in hopes of finding a place where I could find an Internet café. I needed to talk with Marynia. Nothing else mattered. It had been too many days since the last contact, and I knew she would be frantic with worry. Yet for all the pressing on, the next village didn't have an Internet connection available for use.

That night, depression stalked me. I wrote in the journal:

> *"I had lost the smile that I had found earlier that day on the trail. I again began to feel sorry for myself, angry at others. For a while in the morning I thought I finally had gotten it all together. I was sad, losing hope and blaming the world. I wanted the walk to save me; I wanted Marynia to save me; I wanted analysis to save me. None of it was working. I blamed my parents, the priests who molested me, my grandfather. So many people had hurt me as I grew up, even as an adult. I wanted them all to somehow fix me, take responsibility for my depression, for my loss of hope, for the darkness that haunted me."*

The next morning, I walked on, feeling totally exhausted for having slept badly. I felt a strange sense of being more at peace with myself. The only anxiety that remained, was of being able to find an Internet connection to let Marynia and the children know that I was okay, perhaps even better than okay.

By the time I got to Figeac late that afternoon, I knew I couldn't walk any further. My feet were in too much pain. Yet, rather than go to the hostel to rest and care for my feet, I wandered around the city centre in search of Internet. I finally found Internet service in a computer store just before the store was about to close. I talked with Marynia for more than an hour, even after the owner of the shop had closed his place for the evening. He had seen my tears as I wrote messages to her. The owner didn't have the heart to interrupt the scene playing out."

Her: Where are you?

me: I am in Figeac, ahead of my schedule

Her: Ok. Expected an e-mail from Conques, so was so worried.

me: If you promise to do the second half with me, the Spain part, I will go home when I finish the France part, in three more weeks.

Her: I promise with all my heart.

me: We could do it in two years from now

Her: This is too hard apart. You decide when, I promise to come.

me: I will plan when and where I will quit this lonely walk so that we can do it together.

Her: Ok, quit tomorrow would be great for me, but I will wait for you, that I promise. I miss you more than life itself, but I want you to heal and decide what is best for you.

me: It won't be long, believe me. [September 11, 2012]

The next morning, I left the hostel early, in search of answers. I wandered streets in the pale light of dawn. Eventually I found a tiny café that was open where I ate a small breakfast. I sat in silence without being forced to talk with other pilgrims. I had left the hostel without saying any goodbyes to the pilgrims who had become my friends on the trail. I sat and wondered if I was going to walk the rest of the trail to Saint Jean Pied de Port, or if I was going to go home. The time spent in the café stretched longer than normal as I ordered more coffee. A decision had been made. The Camino in France was done. It was time to go home.

Chapter Twenty-Six – Through a Naturist Lens

A private place for meditation at home, November 2012.

I returned home from France a changed man. I knew I wasn't completely healed; however, I had put a lot of ghosts of the past to rest. The stop in Conques and the experiences in the Cathedral had been a significant part of that healing. A long and difficult journey still lay ahead. Another different kind of pilgrimage was yet to be walked, one that would be a shared journey with Marynia. While I wrote about the pilgrimage in France, we planned for a winter of warmth in Central America. A short stay in Mexico would be followed by the remainder of the winter spent in Belize.

It didn't take me long to set up a meditation corner in my home office, a sacred space. I returned to meditating nude in that sacred space. Meditation on the Camino had been done clothed out of necessity. Nude meditation felt more honest, a complete immersion into a state of sacredness.

Nudity continued to challenge my belief systems. I bounced back and forth between the two extremes of wearing clothes and being clothing free. I had hoped that I could have somehow walked away from nudity and returned to a normal life. First there was too much nudity, and then no nudity at all. As it began to be evident that no nudity left me very agitated, Marynia suggested that I keep nudity in my life, as long as it was kept private. Neither of us understood why the need to be nude, but life was better for us if my nudity was given its time and place.

I began to again take naturism seriously. And, as was always the case when I decided to look at things in depth, I turned to Jungian psychology to look for answers. Jungian psychology was the lens through which I hoped to come to grips with this compulsion for nudity. That decision lead to the rebirth of a new blog site, Through a Naturist Lens.

I needed to come clean in the world, to be honest with myself and others. This need for transparency, to be authentic, became something vital to the process of healing post-Camino. And, I had Marynia's support. I chose to begin looking at naturism as a form of alchemy, psychological alchemy, a process that allows a person to deal with the trauma of the past, trauma that continued to hold a person as a hostage to the past. Bit by bit, the threads that bind one to past trauma are exorcised, burnt away. I shared this naturist and psychological approach to transformational change on both of my blog sites.

I began to reinvent myself, to transform my life through a blending of naturism, Jungian psychology, and Buddhist meditation. At the same time, our house was being renovated with new siding, windows and doors. It was synchronicity; two seemingly unrelated activities mirrored each other. As I changed, so did our physical home. Our home, like all homes, was the outer world symbol of our union as a couple. Because I had changed, we changed. As Marynia changed, there became more room for me to move on to the next stage of transformational work, of healing body, mind and soul. The interconnectedness between us, a conscious choice to remain together and work life out together, demanded that both of us become more aware of each other and to risk the changes that were yet to come.

> *"As I meditate nude, there is a blossoming of energy that touches the roots of my body as well as my mind which embraces so much more that what I should know. And as I am awakened to this 'Bindu,' I experience a freedom that far surpasses that of simply being clothes free. I feel the fullness of being a man, the fullness of being a child of the god and goddess of all creation."* [December 12, 2012]

I felt healthier, mentally and physically healthier, when I meditated nude. It was a moment of pure honesty, no cover-ups, no masks, nothing to hide behind, and no need to hide that truth.

The renovation work on the house in Saskatchewan was completed only days before it was time to leave for our winter stay in Latin America.

> *"In just a few hours I will be on a plane heading south to a warmer place. I have booked a studio suite in Puerto Morelos just a few steps away from the Caribbean Sea. Actually, the studio is located about two kilometres north of the town, a more secluded location, a quieter location. I wonder what changes will occur in me over these months away from my*

home in Canada. How will my relationship with M be transformed as I am transformed? This is a shared journey, not only a winter get-away, but to a continually changing future of our relationship."
[January 8, 2013]

We left Canada for Mexico, and a small fishing village called Puerto Morelos. Our arrival into warmth and sunshine was a celebration, a return that was not under the same dark cloud that had existed several years earlier when we travelled to Latin America.

From our tiny condo, we walked along the beach to the village, which lay two kilometres away. We had to pass a nudist resort where couples were nude on the beach and in their lounge chairs, as we made the walk to the town. A bit further down the beach towards the town, before the main beach, we saw another couple laying naked beside the sea, sunbathing. This was unexpected, a shock. I had always believed that nudity was a private activity, not a public activity. I didn't remember beach nudity from when I was a teenager in Ottawa.

Somehow, the idea of sex got in the way; a belief that one only was naked in public as an exhibitionist. Yet, here we saw ordinary people, naked in full view, tanning as if there was nothing shameful about being nude in public. Shame existed only in the minds of those passing by, those who blushed at the nudity in front of their eyes. Shame was a state of mind, not a state of clothing.

Even though that realisation confronted me, I continued to hide my body while meditating nude. It was only when Marynia pointed out some relatively private spots along the beach nearer the nudist resort where I could sunbathe, when I was finally able to take nudity outside of the studio. She reminded me of my nude meditations in the Philippines. Hearing her, I finally gave my self permission.

It was hard, for deep in the background there were echoes from the world of the Catholic Church telling me nudity was a sin. Being nude might not be a sin but being nude so that others could see you was a sin. Nudity was about sex, and that was that as far as the world understood nudity. I knew better, but that fundamentalist beast within me said otherwise. I dared to create a safe spot along that stretch of the Caribbean Sea. I sunbathed between the sea and private land guarded by a fence. I lay in the sunshine, in a shallow basin beside bushes hiding me from the eyes of passing beach walkers.

Marynia tried to understand. Why did I need to be nude? Why did I need to be naked when the rest of the world, the civilised world, was doing quite well with their clothing on? I attempted an answer through a new blog post at the Naturist Lens blog site.

"This morning, I opened up the door to the question during my time for meditation which then lasted longer than usual. It was essential to let the question stew for a while, allow the contents within to become stirred up in the darkness of the unconscious.

As a child I was sexually abused, emotionally abused, and physically abused in my family of origin by my biological parents. The sexual abuse extended to include my maternal grandfather and more than one parish priest.

It was soon after the sexual abuse from my maternal grandfather, the last time I was sexually abused as a youth, I found myself in a quiet meadow in a nearby small forest with a book of poetry. It was a warm late spring day, about six months following this last incidence. Feeling the warmth of the sun and feeling the words of classical poetry, I soon found myself naked. Over the next two years, my last two years at home, I took every opportunity, weather permitting to hide in this forest and meadow in order to be free.

Yet now, the pull to nudity is again strong, so I look to these roots and it dawned on me that it is being nude where I claimed control of my body, control of my identity, control of my sexuality. My body is not about pleasing others, making life easier for others. It comes down to control. Am I in control or do I defer control to someone else?

Now, in my sixties, I am saying, this is my body and I will care for it, and my identity, and my psyche as best I can. I will not be a child and give control to another. I am a man, not a child victim continuing to seek approval, seeking to please others while disregarding myself." [January 25, 2013]

As the end of January approached, and with it the time to relocate to Belize, Marynia showed me a perfect place for nude meditation nearer our studio. She had thought that meditation at the end of a pier would allow me to meditate at the approach of dawn. This was the time I usually meditated, in a natural state. Though it would put me in full view of early morning passersby on the beach, I would be far enough away so that all that would be seen would be my back as I meditated facing the rising sun. The next morning while meditating at the end of that pier for the first time, Marynia took photos if me in meditation facing the rising sun.

Then it was time to leave Puerto Morelos, on a bus to Playa del Carmen, where we took another bus to Corozal, Belize.

-

The ground floor apartment in Corozal, was beautiful and quite large. The garden outside the apartment, faced an abandoned field, which made the garden area very private. I was glad that I wouldn't have to leave that garden in search of a quiet spot near the sea for sunbathing or for dawn meditation. I had my own sacred garden in which I could continue to do the work of healing sky clad. Wrapped in nothing but the air, sky clad, I focused on breathing and releasing old pain.

I meditated, sunbathed, wrote blog posts, and read during this journey of healing in Belize. Together with Marynia, we went walking daily, learning about the community, and taking photographs. There was no pressure to do more than this. Feeling the tensions of the past loosen, life together became better. The journey to Corozal had begun to show its purpose. I wrote:

> *Few know that I meditate, none have seen me meditate, and perhaps even fewer would accept the idea of meditation while sky clad. I have become aware of the shift of behaviour from shadow behaviour to conscious behaviour, purposeful rather than reactive. I now live as fully and honestly as I can."* [February 9, 2013]

Finally, with a sense of place in the town of Corozal, we began to explore beyond the borders of the town. Exploration had stopped being an act of escape, a way to flee from being too much together and reacting out of too-much-ness. We explored to learn and experience Belize.

Before our time in Corozal came to an end, we both had decided to return to Puerto Morelos and the long beach, if it was even possible, rather than to go on to the next place I had booked in Belize. The next lodging in Belize was cancelled and we booked ten days in Playa del Carmen before returning to stay in Puerto Morelos. The remaining days in Belize became even more relaxed knowing that we would soon be returning to Puerto Morelos.

In Playa del Carmen, my mood remained positive as the beach was beautiful, perfect for long daily walks. At the end of the beach, away from the city, we had discovered a tiny, private space among the rocks, where being nude wouldn't be an issue. That secluded corner allowed me to add to a growing collection of photos for a book of poetry that had begun to take shape in my mind. The ten days in Playa del Carmen went by quickly. We left Playa with positive memories and returned to Puerto Morelos.

Unable to rent the condo we had lived in a month earlier, we found a new place in Puerto Morelos, the back section of a house called Casa Sorpresas. This was the first year that the studio apartment had been offered for rent. The studio suited us perfectly, especially because of the sunny garden area surrounded by high walls where I again had a secret garden, a sacred space.

Living in the community of Puerto Morelos exceeded our expectations. We had the best of living in town without losing the beach and the kilometres of sand for daily two-hour beach walks. Along with daily walks around the town, I spent time writing in the garden. The privacy of the garden allowed me to write without needing to wear clothes. The writing began to focus more and more on poetry than it did about writing blog posts. I was being transformed by the constant sunshine.

This was the beginning of writing while nude, the final element in this journey of healing. I was daring to tell my story, telling the whole, naked truth without holding back because I was afraid to offend others. It was time for transparency and honesty. It was time for me to stop asking permission, always trying to second guess what others wanted, trying to fit into those expectations. Telling my story, exposing everything, was all about setting the context of where I came from and how I survived extensive childhood trauma. I wrote to allow others to finally get to know who I really was. It was at this time that the Naturist Lens blog site shifted in terms of self-disclosure. I began to post images that were more personal, taking an even greater risk with being honest about who I was.

One of the risks I took without realising that it was a risk, was in taking my nude meditation into the garden area. As the weeks had gone by, the sense of privacy within the garden allowed me to feel invulnerable. This garden was my safe place. I continued to go to sunbathing near the clothing optional beach, but meditation, as well as writing, was saved for this secret garden.

With just a few weeks remaining in our stay at Casa Sorpresas, the woman who had rented out the studio to us, walked into the garden while I was meditating. She saw that I was nude and silently retreated. She returned a short while later when meditation was almost done. She came with a gift which she presented to me, a deck of cards that featured her mother's art work. I was still sitting on the meditation cushion, nude with only an edge of the towel covering me. She ignored my nudity. She then asked if we wanted to rent the studio again for the following winter. It felt as if I had just passed a test. Though seeing me nude, she was willing to have us back as seasonal renters.

We booked for two months at Casa Sorpresas for the following winter. We would have to find a place for January as the owner of the studio had already booked that month to someone else. For the remainder of our time in Puerto Morelos, we both relaxed with the knowledge of returning to this same village and the same studio for the next year.

Chapter Twenty-Seven – Green Haven

Green Haven Sun Club,
a naturist retreat to write and decompress, June 2013.

Life returned to a tentative, new normal back in Saskatchewan. It was a newer, shifting, and constantly changing normal. The Marynia and Robert who had left Canada in January had both changed. And, we were continuing to change even more with the passing of time. Despite the cool, spring, prairie weather, my naturist tendencies remained with nude meditation, and braving the cool spring weather while being sky clad on the prairie hills on rare occasions.

"A few months ago, I posted why I have shifted my life to include being nude at opportune times – at home, in private nature spaces and along clothing-optional stretches of beach. Nothing has changed since that post other than the sense that my need for being clothing free seems to be stronger than ever. Not only do I feel that naturism is part of my healing process, I also have begun to experience joy. Simply being without clothing brings a sense of lightness to

*my spirit. It is as though I have escaped from a locked
box in which the universe is darker and sadder. Who
wouldn't want to feel more joyful in their lives?"*
[May 11, 2013]

So, now all that I needed to do was to fit naturism into my
life in Canada without offending others. I knew I didn't live
within a bubble. The real world was either absolutely
opposed to nudity, indifferent, or simply quite wary of those
who chose to be nude. People have been socially
programmed to be fearful of nudists and naturists, afraid of
their intentions. I had no intention of having my nudity break
family bonds or friendship bonds. I didn't know with whom
being nude would be the factor that would bring an end to
any given relationship. During this time of testing of
boundaries, Marynia was on edge. She feared that I would
cross a line that would then impact on her community and
family relationships. Tension began to creep back into our
lives.

What remained the same was a shared commitment to family
and community friends, as they began the regular round of
visiting and being visited in return. Near the end of May, we
went to visit a few people who were part of the Prairie Suns
Naturist club near North Battleford. It was a small event with
just three others including the host couple. An afternoon in
the sunshine was spent with our hosts. We left after a potluck
supper, having made new friends. I didn't know how we
could maintain this friendship, and have it become part of our
larger life because of nudity. Marynia, though not afraid of
being nude, preferred to wear clothing.

I began disclosing more and more of my life history on the
Naturist Lens blog site, old stuff and new realisations. I
began to understand more of what could only be called,
naturist spiritualism. Synchronicity lead me to find a web site
by Ed Raby Sr, called "All Things Rabyd." The author of the
site was a Protestant pastor who wrote on various spiritual

and religious themes. Tucked into a part of this web site were articles that discussed the topic, "God and Nudity." There were quite a few articles that investigated the spiritual value of nakedness. The articles spoke at length about the holiness of being "Naked before God." Pastor Raby talked about nakedness in both physical and spiritual terms and showed how the two blended together.

As I read, I began to let go of the Catholic idea that nudity was sin. By approaching naturism as a spiritual practice, I began to give up the idea that being naked was a perversion. Being sky clad was okay and perhaps, even a holy way of being present in the world.

As my allergies had continued to be a problem, I had decided to continue with the series of allergy treatments I had begun in Toronto. Marynia located a treatment centre in Estevan, a five-hour drive from our home. A commitment made to following up the initial treatments I had begun years earlier in Toronto. Because of its proximity to the Green Haven Sun Club, I decided, with the support of Marynia, to go to the naturist site following treatments rather than make the return five-hour trip home the same day. The treatments usually left me quite tired, too tired to safely drive into the evening. We talked about my going to Green Haven as being a wellness retreat

So, began a new chapter in my life as a naturist, the world of sharing naturism with other naturists. In early June 2013, I went to Green Haven for the first time. In my journal, I wrote:

"So far, it is quiet with only a few people tucked into their trailers because of the coolness of the weather. In spite of that coolness, I am reluctant to go back into my trailer because of the sunshine even though it is weak and not "warming." It is the thought that counts. With the prediction of cloudy and rainy

weather for the next few days, this is as good as it is going to get.

I have learned something from Buddhism, to be present in the moment and not focused on the past or the future. The present has sunshine and a brisk breeze, and I am outside – naked. Life is good." [June 13, 2013]

The journal continued, explaining:

"Nudity is too important to me at this time to risk having it sabotage my healing. Nudity is a major aspect of my healing journey, a way of washing away the sins of the past committed upon me and committed by me. Feeling the heat of the sun almost cook me, is best described as being in an alchemist's cauldron being changed and transformed and purified. I will go into that more at another time. It is enough now, to say that as I lay in the sunshine, totally present with the rays and the heat and in my body, I feel a healing stirring within me. In a way, it felt as though I was being washed and cleansed, being purified by light. As I said before, this all has the feel of a spiritual journey." [June 13]

That first solitary visit to Green Haven had taught me a lot about being whole as I lived without clothing for a few days in spite of the cool weather. During that time, I found the courage to dig deep within and confront various fears that continued to linger. I read, I wrote, and I breathed deeply. I knew that I would return to Green Haven, alone if necessary. I needed this freedom to be without clothing, rather than live with the fear of what others would say about me.

'Where is all this nudity taking me? And, how is it affecting Marynia?' I was caught somewhere between being authentically myself and living an increasingly artificial life with family and community. I could sense a tenseness in the

air each time I was nude at home. Boundaries became an ongoing issue. Where and when could I be nude, was constantly being negotiated and re-negotiated, usually on a non-verbal level. Each time I cut back too much on being nude, I would get very agitated and there would be a corresponding response to that agitation by Marynia. When I was too much nude, she got agitated and there would be a corresponding response to that agitation by me. This bouncing back and forth set off each other's triggers which activated our respective complexes. It was a very uncomfortable dance.

Near the end of June, I returned to Green Haven. Going alone meant that I got to be nude as many hours as I chose within the campgrounds. The benefit was that Marynia was insulated from having to deal with my nudity. Returning to Green Haven alone was an attempt to give both of us what we needed, a solution that met both of sets of needs.

> *"When Marynia sends me off to do what I need to do to get healed, I wonder if this naturism process is part of the solution or simply a diversion in keeping me at a safe distance from what I need to deal with."* [June 25, 2013]

I didn't really know the answers to the questions now popping up in my head. My intuition told me one thing, and my ego told me the opposite. What was evident was that the journey of healing was still in process.

On the third trip to Green Haven, I wasn't alone. In relationships that hope to last, it is vital to find a way to try and understand the other person in the relationship. With understanding, choices become based on reason rather than being reactions out of fear. Marynia was with me.

> *"While walking this morning, Marynia was talking about those she has met and the others whom she has heard about from the lady who takes care of*

registrations. She noted that it appears that almost everyone at Green Haven appears to be wounded in some way, making Green Haven more of a naturist retreat centre than a naturist club. Since I referred to my initial visits here as engaging in a naturist retreat of one person, her idea made a lot of sense." [July 10, 2013]

For a few days, Marynia shared in my practice naturism and nudity, including interactions with others who were also nude. We didn't talk about what to do or not do, both just became fully present in that small nudist community, and fully present to each other and those with whom we interacted.

After five full days at Green Haven, it was time to return to everyday life. Following the stay at Green Haven, we went on a two-week tour visiting extended family, distant friends, and hiking. For those two weeks, depression and shadows became distant memories. I was present, positive, and enjoyed the days away from home. I had continued to write in the quiet moments found along the way, and I didn't feel anxious when those moments didn't appear with any regularity. Then we returned home.

"Today is not such a good day in the grand scheme of things for me. Every once in a while, I crash and find myself having to pick up the pieces and put them back together again like some senior citizen Humpty Dumpty. After two weeks of putting myself out there in a fairly active manner, I simply had run out of energy. That is one of the problems of being an introvert." [July 30, 2013]

I needed time to withdraw and recharge my internal battery. This need wasn't about being wounded, but more about being an introvert. We only had three days at home before grandchildren and their parents were to arrive and spend some quality time with us. It was to be a time for summer fun at the grandparents. The three days had been enough time for me to again be present enough to play and enjoy playing with my grandchildren.

When everyone left, it was time for me to return to Estevan for another allergy treatment and another stay at Green Haven. For the second time, I didn't go alone. With her first time at Green Haven being so positive, I was surprised when conflict erupted, a conflict focused on nudity.

> *"Marynia says she can't change anymore to fit into how I am changing. If we are to survive as a couple, there is not much room for naturism. I need to become less of a loner, I need to fit better into community making it easier for her in the community. As her pain spilled out with tears, I sat stunned. I didn't react with off the wall anger or self-critical comments which had been my typical response in the past. I let her words sit there, heavy. I was too taken aback to process this information in terms of what next."* [August 14, 2013]

Before the summer was over, I made one more trip to Green Haven, alone. I had retreated from being nude in front of Marynia at home in hopes of making it easier for her. I hated conflict between us. I didn't want to risk our marriage because of my perceived need to be nude. My head was swirling with the fear that I would somehow slip up and have it all come crashing down. Nudity was kept hidden behind the door of my home office where I continued to write and meditate while nude.

-

As autumn approached, Marynia began to talk more and more about walking the Camino together as she had promised me a year earlier. With a plan to walk the Camino agreed upon, we decided to spend a few days in Saskatoon hiking the Meewasin Trails, testing our bodies, and to see what more was needed in terms of training and equipment. We set our sights for walking the Camino for the fall of 2015. We wanted to be prepared, physically and mentally, for that challenge of walking eight hundred kilometres.

Summer had left me feeling physically better than I had felt for years. The intensity of my seasonal allergies had retreated. As I looked back over the summer, I had to admit that the attention to meditation, writing and to naturism, with an active program of allergy treatments and hiking, had been a good part of why it had been the best summer I had experienced for many, many years. I also realised that the work in Calgary with analysis, and the walk through a part of France on the Camino had also been significant contributing factors to my improved mental and physical health. Was I healed? No, there was no fixing the past. I was still healing. I was still learning to cope better.

I had begun to write poetry again in the fall of 2013, naturist poetry that I had begun writing while we were in Mexico. I had the intention of publishing a book of poetry. Writing was therapy for me, as much as meditation and naturism were therapies. In the Jungian Lens blog site, I wrote:

> "*I take photographs and I write. These two things have likely done much for my finding and maintaining a decent level of mental health. Both photography and writing help bring balance to my life. I don't write to figure things out, I write, and things straighten themselves out below my level of conscious awareness.*" [September 27, 2013]

Writing had become a focal point of my day, as much as had meditation. Both were being done while I was nude. I didn't know it at the time, but I was apprenticing for a larger task, the work that would become a series of books that would tell my story. This is the final book in that series. For the present, I began to put the poetry I had written, into book format.

The book was published as <u>Naked Poetry: By the Sea and on the Prairies</u>. I then turned my attention towards the writing of a novel for the National Novel Writing Month, [NaNoWriMo] project, hoping that I could write a 50,000-word novel in thirty days during the month of November. With the poetry book completed, I began to write a practice novel to see if I had it within me to write consistently at the required pace. As I wrote, it became difficult to separate truth from fiction. It seemed no matter what I wrote, a part of me seemed to slip into the story.

> *"So, what is the "real" story of our lives? Are they all real or all unreal, all provisional? There are the stories we tell ourselves, and the stories we tell others. Some of them may even be true. But what are the stories which are storying their way through our daily lives and of which we are mostly if not wholly unaware? What are the stories that represent our rationalizations, our defenses, the stories in which we remain stuck like flies in molasses?"*

Reading this in part of a book sent to me by James Hollis, a Jungian analyst and author, I decided to base the novel I was going to write, on the story of how I had come to meet Marynia. It would be a fictional only in terms of the names of characters and the dialogue between characters. The plot would tell the real story. I had never written about any of this part of my life in the past. I had firmly believed that there was no need, that this story was too private. Even when it came to writing-as-therapy, journaling-as-therapy, I had avoided telling this story. However, everything had changed within me. The old prohibitions that had me keep the past hidden had begun to dissolve. That novel, <u>On The Broken Road</u>, was finished in less than a month. The book was to eventually become the second book in the series.

Then I began the process of editing the novel, listening to both my inner critic and to the voice of Marynia who had highlighted those areas which made her feel uncomfortable. I listened and berated myself for having spoken in the novel in ways that seemed to cause more harm than good. I was ready to burn the book as I had burnt so many of my writings in the past. The resulting storm between us passed as it had always passed. I took Marynia's ideas and reworked the book. Scenes were deleted, conversation was stripped of offensive language, and what remained was approached with more care in the retelling the tale. In the end, the novel became ten thousand words longer. And more importantly, it was better.

I sent my siblings and our children eBook versions of the two books I had written, the naturist poetry book as well as the novelized autobiography. Both books had been also published and available for sale with a print-on-demand service. Now, all I had to do was wait for the royalties to pour in. As expected, our children were quick to tell me that they liked the novel. What was unexpected was the response from some of my brothers and sisters. Those who wrote were very supportive, pleased to have been included in the novel as characters, and I was even more surprised that what I had said in the novel had matched what they saw as the truth about our family-of-origin.

The novel showed the darkness, and the primary role of nudity in escaping that darkness in the span of just one year of my life. As I wrote, the pieces in my head had begun to be pulled into some sort of order. I knew what still needed to be done, the telling of the story of the first twenty years of my life. I would have to write that book next. It would become the first book in the Journey of Healing series.

Chapter Twenty-Eight – What is Acceptable Changes

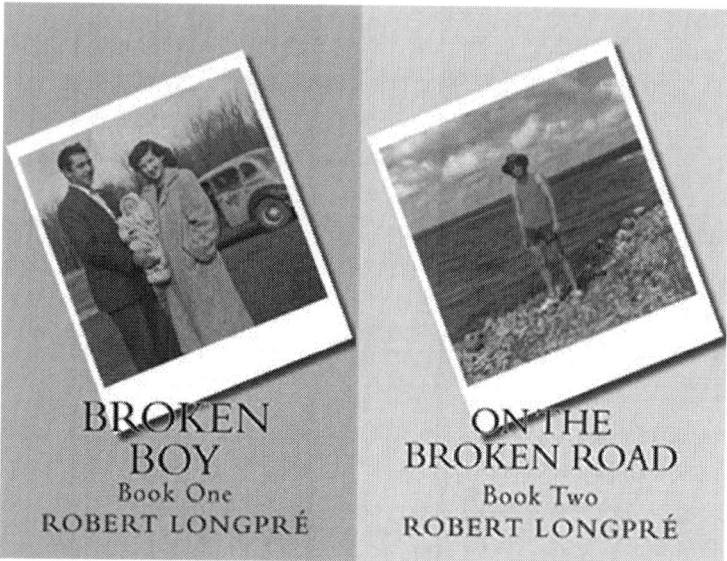

With the novel On The Broken Road completed, I found it difficult to return again to reading, meditation, and to a full outer life. Too much had been activated within me with the writing of the memoir novel. Strangely, instead of euphoria, I was again depressed and super-sensitive. An underlying depression that had more to do with a seasonal darkness, than it did with pressing shadows, had settled in. Rather than write about my first twenty years of life, I wanted to write a follow-up story to the novel, the third part of my life. However, the words which would have become that story, simply refused to be written. It would take years before this book would be published in this final edition.

By Christmas 2013, life became energised with family and friends filling in the silences. There were no thoughts of naturism, Jungian psychology, or Buddhism. However, just before the New Year I began writing a lengthy blog post at Jungian Lens about nudism. It was a post Marynia said needed to be shared. It was important to her that others understood why I, her husband, was behaving so differently, why I felt compelled to write so much about naturism on my blog site.

"This is a hard piece of writing to bring out of my mind so that you can read it and perhaps understand a bit more of who I am and why I am the way I am ... I am a stranger to myself as much as I am to everyone else; and in a way, that has been a deliberate strategy I have used throughout my life to protect myself and hopefully protect those around me from the dark, dank and dangerous stuff that lies buried deep within me ... The past haunts me. Traumatic events leave a permanent mark on those who are traumatized. The trauma is coded into both the body and the psyche, that inner, intangible part of self ... PTSD – post traumatic stress disorder.

Trauma has a way of working its way out of its imprisonment [within the psyche]. All it takes are triggers. ... I am damaged goods. I have become a conscious naturist and Buddhist as part of my healing journey. This is who I am, and I accept it ... I can't change my past. I can't undo the damage I have done on my journey to get to today. But I can understand and accept and find compassion for myself and for others". [December 29, 2013]

The response to the post by both family and friends told me that the risking of disclosing his early history was worth the angst and the fear of being too vulnerable. With that blog post, and with the novel made available to the public, I began to learn more from siblings and cousins about my family-of-origin history, things that I had never even suspected to have happened. And, I began to dread what yet would be revealed of my own story. I had opened locked doors and stuff was still pouring out from all sorts of directions. More than anything else, these messages confirmed within me that I had not been creating false memories. Others saw what I saw, and sometimes they saw more.

And then it was time to fly off to Mexico.

-

We arrived in Playa del Carmen and settled into an apartment called Casa Verde. Life in Playa became a time of sunshine and warmth, taking the place of the fierce cold left behind in Canada. Since we had been in Playa del Carmen the year before, we quickly found a routine. We roamed the beaches, and along Fifth Avenue, and walked until we were too tired to walk any more. Fatigue was the antidote to thinking and feeling too much.

The ghosts exposed days before our departure from Canada had left both of us ultra-sensitive. The oppressive feelings that surfaced had set me on edge. A week after our arrival, I again took down the Naturist Lens blog site. I blamed Marynia. Then, out of guilt for having unfairly blamed her, I turned my anger and frustration onto myself for being so obsessed with nudity.

I again deleted photos and my journal. It was as if by destroying all of it, I would be burning out whatever it was that caused so much pain. I blamed it all on nudity rather than the writing of my story that had awakened old trauma. I was afraid of what was bubbling inside of him, afraid of that stuff being projected onto Marynia. More than anything, it felt like there wasn't room anymore for me to be different. I began to believe that if we were to survive as a couple, I had to become someone different, someone normal.

With these self-defeating thoughts laying waste to my confidence, I gave up meditation completely and made sure that I wrote only while clothed. My complexes had been triggered, which in turn had triggered Marynia's complexes.

It appeared as if there was no way to survive the ongoing storms.

"The shoe that fits one person, pinches another; there is no universal recipe for living. Each of us carries his own life-form within him – an irrational form which no other can outbid."

I was pinching, trying to fit into a way of being that didn't fit anymore. Trying as hard as I could, I couldn't simply adapt. As the heat settled, we both became more careful with each other and around each other. The problem was that neither of us were being authentic or honest with each other. Both became victims of trying too hard to fit into the shoes of the other. Both were walking on eggshells hoping to avoid triggering yet another storm.

"Like anyone else, I wanted to be in full control of myself and hated it when I wasn't in control, when it felt like others had control over me. Not realising that this lack of control usually had its roots within myself, I was quick to lay blame on others for stealing control from me. [January 19, 2014]

Control issues were at the heart of these silent conflicts, and that control conflict was centred on the issue of change. It looked and felt like the other partner had become a stranger. What was left, was the feeling of having lost the person we had married and loved over the years.

Too much effort had been given to contain the past, to disguise it and hide that past. I had hidden and denied critical parts of me, which then had almost destroyed me and our marriage. I was ruled by the fear of losing Marynia. But at greater risk was the fear of losing myself.

I didn't know this, consciously – no one ever does. The more one truly believes that they know themselves one hundred percent, the more they are a victim of the denied parts of themselves. Between Marynia and me, the control issue had shifted to focus on nudity and normalcy.

Three weeks into the New Year, the inner self pull drew me back into nudity, at least on an intellectual level. It reappeared on the Jungian Lens blog site. I soon was twisting and turning in the posts at Through a Jungian Lens. It didn't matter that I had shut down the Naturist Lens site, the exposure of self through words continued, the wrestling with self-identity was highlighted.

The sequel to the novel On The Broken Road, was abandoned as I just wasn't ready to tell that story, nor was Marynia ready for it to be told. I had to settle my debts with the ghosts of those first twenty years of life. Marynia had recognised that I was again slipping backwards, slipping into a depression with my attempts at disowning nudity. With her encouragement, I regained enough balance to make peace with this unconscious need for nudity before we moved back to Puerto Morelos.

The first week back in Puerto Morelos was hot. We went walking along the beach for hours and then went for a swim in the sea. I would then go sunbathing by the sea in the secluded sand dunes. Writing was set aside for the most part as we readjusted to living again in Puerto Morelos. It was time to let the sun and the privacy of the little garden even out the rough edges that had been exposed in Playa del Carmen.

> "I am quieter than normal, and a good part of that quietness is due to being caught in the swirling waters of depression, denying the depression and as a result, causing myself and my life partner too much grief in the process. It is hard to see 'self' in any kind of good light when depression re-enters the picture."
> [February 11, 2014]

I now felt the need to begin telling that story of abuse that marked my first twenty years of life, and so I began to write. Without thinking about it, I began slipping into being nude more often. Writing while nude was as much a part of the writing process, as was the keyboard of the laptop. Nudity had become intertwined with the letting go of the dark images that emerged. I was finally beginning to accept that reality.

The story consumed me. I wrote and exposed new memories, I found backed-upped material hidden in old file folders that had survived the attempted purges, files unconsciously protected from those irrational moments of 'burn and destroy." I had found enough of the story which became the foundation for the retelling.

I decided that I couldn't turn the story into a novel though I did keep the names of the characters fictitious, the same names that had been used in <u>On The Broken Road</u>. I wrote the truth, as I knew it while growing up. If the book was going to be read by others, such as my brothers and sisters who knew a good part of the story, they deserved to hear the truth.

"It wasn't long ago that I believed that it was important to keep the peace, even if that meant not speaking about something that needed to be said ... This avoidance of exposing ghosts and setting them free only allowed those phantoms of the mind and memory to dominate the inner spaces of myself, ensuring that inner peace would never become a reality ... And so, I now find myself too tired to play this game. I haven't done anyone any justice in keeping a smile on my face and keeping the peace ... Now it's time for me to stop hiding, stop disguising, and stop trying so hard to please others by twisting myself like a pretzel into shapes that would please them. It's time to risk being vulnerable and being

patient, about accepting without judgment the fact of who I am and how I am in this world." [February 20, 2014]

While in Mexico, during the last month of our winter getaway, I had begun to relax again. Nudity seemed to have become less and less of a problem. I began to think that Marynia had finally become more comfortable with my nudity, not realising that it was me who had become more comfortable with nudity.

-

During the spring of 2014 our focus turned to the Camino which was planned for the autumn of 2015. It was time to focus energies on developing confidence through training. As well as the focus on the Camino, I continued to write poetry. He also continued to work on the story of being a broken boy child. I had written quite a few poems while in Playa del Carmen and Puerto Morelos, perhaps enough for the second book of poetry. But I wanted to have more poetry so that there would be choice when it was time to gather the poems together for another poetry book. My naturist wanderings in the prairie hills had provided me with new material for the poetry collection.

After an absence of three months, I decided to revive the Naturist Lens blog site.

"I have been gone from this site for almost as long as I was in Mexico. In fact, I thought that the site had completely disappeared. It was a message from my host server reminding me to update the WordPress software that I used that made me realise that this place was still in existence though it wasn't visible to the world. A few clicks and the renaming of a file soon had this site re-appear so that I could talk again with you. Is this a good thing or not?" [April 11, 2014]

I felt relief at discovering I hadn't destroyed everything I had written, though I was uncertain enough of Marynia's reaction to the restoration of the blog site. I kept silent about the revival of the blog site, though Marynia had encouraged its existence in the past. She had even protested its destruction in Playa. I also stayed silent about its revival for I didn't know if it would survive long enough to risk any sort of reaction. The element of trust in myself was in question. I didn't want another slash and destroy mission to upset her as it had the last time. I just wasn't willing to risk disturbing the peace between us that had since re-emerged. I kept the writing, meditation, and time spent nude in a separate, safe, and solitary world.

Near the end of April 2014, I was beginning to psychologically thaw out, as the first of pleasant spring weather began to make an appearance. My whole being opened as though it had just been released from solitary confinement. I became happier despite a return of seasonal allergies.

With the warmer days of late spring and early summer, nature became my Cathedral, becoming a spiritual world. Inner darkness was banished during those holy moments in nature while I was nude. With the easing of spirit, it became easier for Marynia and me to be with each other, finding enjoyment again in being together.

The Camino took over most of our attention. We both read the Camino adventures of other people, we hiked at every opportunity when weather allowed, and tested out hiking gear. There was a belief that we were finally going to do this, walk the Camino.

My allergies were a problem that just didn't seem to go away with summer approaching. Marynia suggested that I to return for allergy treatments. The plan that evolved, would be for me to make retreat stops at Green Haven with each scheduled appointment, but somehow life got in the way of these naturist retreats and I felt the loss of self-promised naturist time at Green Haven keenly. Weather was the main reason for canceling the stays at the naturist club near Regina. With her needs met as I contained nudity to safe times and places, we became more relaxed. The tension eased. The release of tensions in turn gave me more space for being nude. My nudity seemed to be becoming more acceptable to others as well. It was early July when an event confirmed his sense that being nude in his home was okay in the eyes of others.

"I was sitting in my usual chair, reading, while Marynia sat nearby, talking on the phone, when one of our neighbour friends, Faye who had visited us in China and in Puerto Morelos with her husband, Cameron, quietly entered our house. Usually, when she entered our home, she would call out as she knew that I was often nude. She has seen me naked numerous times, especially those times when she didn't call out.

She entered our living room where I sat reading while nude. Marynia was reading on the sofa to the right of my chair. Faye sat in the rocking chair immediately to the left of my chair. Then, she handed me a piece of paper. She asked me to write out the rules for a card game she intended to play with her grandchildren while camping. The fact that I was nude made no difference to her. It was as if being nude was normal and acceptable. I was surprised and quite worried about how Marynia would respond.

Marynia told me that the rules were in the cabinet in the dining room. I hesitated to get up and get them. I thought about how it would look to see my genitals swaying back and forth while walking to the cabinet with Faye walking beside me. Sensing my hesitancy and discomfort, Marynia went to the cabinet where the games were stored, calling for Faye to go with her. With the rules finally written out, our neighbour left with a thank you. I guess we now have a new "normal" in our home." [July 7, 2014]

Nothing was said following this event about what had happened, and life went as if nothing unusual had happened. Camping, hiking, studying about the Camino, visiting, being visited, reading, and writing marked the remainder of the summer. With an active increase in camping and engaging in long and longer hikes, life was good. The story being written of my life as a child was ending. My periods of sadness began to recede. Those feelings of sadness had to do with the writing of the story.

On October 7th, I gave Marynia the last chapter to proofread. The book had been written. Dorian was also reading this final version to find errors that need to be addressed before the book was published. A Broken Boy on the Broken Road, was published on October 22nd, as an eBook. Like the first book, it was given away.

Chapter Twenty-Nine – A Shared Project for Poetry

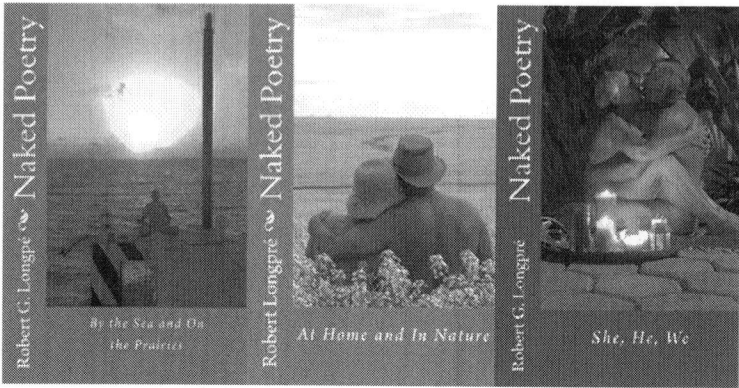

As I wrote during the autumn and early winter, I had forgotten the reasons for engaging in naturism in the first place. I forgot about the therapeutic value of nudity. Nudity had been doing its healing work behind the scenes. By the end of 2014, it seemed as if naturism had become the objective, rather than being part of the healing process. I had begun to simply want to be nude. I had already come a long way from the crash in late 2011 that had sent me back into Jungian analysis. I was now better than he had been for the past fourteen years. Naturism had unconsciously become a vital part of the process that led to a better level of mental health. Marynia didn't understand why, but she knew that my well-being was tied to being able to have time for being nude. Believing that I was now 'fixed,' I began to think that naturism needed a new reason if it was going to remain in my life.

With so many people now reading the stories of my childhood and youth, as well as the two books of poetry, I celebrated because of the thousands of downloads of the e-books. I now felt like a legitimate writer. But, the shadows within told a different story. Within, deep beneath the level of my conscious awareness, I was still a scared and vulnerable boy; a boy who had turned to being nude in nature to unconsciously begin the long, long journey of healing. When it was time to leave again for Mexico. I was in greedy anticipation of the warmth and sunshine. Though I didn't want to admit it, I was also yearning for the chance to be out of my clothes. There was feeling of safety and comfort in the familiar little studio suite in Casa Sorpresas, in Puerto Morelos.

Settling in upon arriving in Puerto Morelos, I began, once again, to write and meditate. While I meditated and wrote, Marynia took photos of me, something she hadn't done often in the past. She asked about the photo plans for the third poetry book which I had been discussing with her. It was obvious to her that some of my agitation was about not working on the poetry which was my primary writing project in Mexico. She approached the topic by talking about the photos for the She part of the book.

Slowly, it dawned on me that she was willing to be the photo model for the section on the feminine psyche, and for the final section on the holy marriage, the We section. She was doing her best to reanimate my spirits. As we talked about the poetry plan, I realised that the poetry book had now become a shared project, a thought that filled me with hope about Marynia becoming a naturist.

Marynia had suggested that we take the photos based on the overall-plan. Then, I would write the poems with the images we would choose. Together we would brainstorm photos scenarios before heading out to take those photos. She was to let me know when her limits had been reached with regards to her nudity. During those retreat moments between photo shoots, I wrote poetry.

Over the period of a month, all the photos were taken to fit the planned sequence of photos for the project. After every photo shoot, we would go over the photos with Marynia making the final choices of which photos would be used. With her final choices made after each shoot, I would then write the poems to fit those chosen photos. When the project finally came to an end, we had created something beautiful together. It appeared to me that somehow nudity had stopped being a divisive issue. I began to believe that we had entered a new phase in our relationship as a couple where nudity was normal.

I had come to believe that 'we' had arrived in this new future in perfect harmony, to a place where there were no more demons, no more shadows lurking in the darkness. But that was far from the truth. Marynia had the honesty and courage to tell him that she was still not a naturist. She had simply acted out of a belief that I needed the project to succeed for my mental well-being. She clearly stated that she had taken her last nude photo of me and that she would not have any more nude photos taken of her. Despite her statements, the afterglow of the poetry project left me hopeful of better times yet to come, better times which included more shared time as naturists.

The rest of our time in Mexico became a time for simply being together. I was coming to understand a bit more about the power of naturism as vital to my well-being. Marynia's confirmation of what she saw when it came to my nudity, had me began to believe that nudity had finally allowed me to heal. The idea of nudity-as-therapy, which I had first thought about during the summer of 2013, returned.

> "The idea of shedding clothing as a part of a therapy practice in a private, safe space has nothing to do with self-gratification, it has nothing to do with sex. In the setting of your sacred space, removing your clothing is a visible note to oneself to be honest, not to hide. There is the key aspect that I have discovered, that of taking the psyche to a time of innocence and trust. For self-therapy to be effective, one must risk

and trust that the risks taken will heal and not harm the "self." [March 23, 2015]

But of course, healing was not just attributed to nudity. Analysis, journaling, meditation, and family were vital to the process.

Before returning home to Canada, I had already begun to organise for the Camino del Santiago. There was a lot of planning still needed. A benefit that grew out of the planning was the focus into the future. We were anxious to get back on track with training and making this shared dream happen. The trick was to not get stuck in the future. We still needed to be able to return to the present.

With the two books about my life now published and available in print form, I ordered enough copies to give away to my family. The autobiography books challenged me in ways that I hadn't expected. It was one thing to have the books as eBooks floating around somewhere in cyberspace, but with them as physical books in my hand, I was left with the question *'Now what am I going to do with them?'*.

Putting my life and secrets onto paper and into books had been a protest against keeping everything neatly hidden away in a closet. The time for hiding and silence was over. The silence had finally been broken, I had hidden in fear and shame. With the help of others, writing, mediation, and naturism, I was finally able to accept that I would be okay even though the scars would likely continue to give me grief from time to time in the future. The books I had written were vital to the process of learning to forgive myself, to letting go of debilitating shame. Now, there were no more secrets.

Not long after the return home to Canada, I got the news that the brother closest to me in age was in the hospital. He wasn't expected to live much longer. I managed to get to the hospital in Edmonton before he passed away. Though we had fought, as brothers always did, we had a bond forged by shared survival in a home filled with abuse. We had travelled separate paths and rarely communicated once gone from our parents' home. Standing at the side of his hospital bed with only the pressure of his hand squeezing mine in response, that distance was erased. Nothing could change the truth that both had shared too much to ever be less than brothers.

> *"As each of us descends into our personal darkness, we lose hope, self-respect, and time to share with those who care about us. With my second brother, I didn't have a chance to say good-bye. With this brother, my first brother, I got that chance."* [April 18, 2015]

Having taken care of my brother's estate as best I could, my life slipped into a quieter place. Marynia had returned to working at the nursing home, while I tried to sort out the past from the present which had come up with my brother's death. Without deliberately planning it, I again headed into the hills where I shed my clothing. Nude, I wrapped myself in the silence of the prairie hills. The sun, once again, was healing me as it had in the past when the pressures began to overwhelm me. Meditation and sunshine, walking and sunshine, all while nude were now entrenched as rituals of healing.

At the end of June, Marynia went with me to Green Haven. Warm weather and good company made the days spent at Green Haven very pleasant. We visited others, took walks around the grounds, read, sunbathed, swam in the pool, and spent private time free of clothing. Life had changed. All the evidence suggested that nudity had stopped being an issue in my life and our marriage.

-

When the books arrived by parcel delivery from the United States, I put the books on sale in the communities of Elrose and Lanigan, the community where he had raised his family.

I then put a copy of the two volumes of my story in the local library.

Offering the books for sale wasn't about making money. I knew I would never sell enough books to make a living at writing. The motive was about being authentic in a way that invited the world to know the truth of the man they had known as principal, teacher, neighbour, friend, or in whatever role they had known me. Getting the books out there was a different sort of nakedness, new a risk that worried me though I wouldn't admit it. Would these books cause the people in the community to distance themselves? Would neighbours and friends now keep their distance because of the stories, which perhaps should have remained hidden?

I felt that I was approaching the edge of the world, that in exposing myself, psychologically naked, I would fall off the edge. However, that fear had nothing to do with reality. No one had abandoned me as neighbour or friend. Rather, the honesty had opened doors that I had never realised were closed. My presence in community had been solely based on my former role in the community as principal. Now, I had become an ordinary person, fallible and flawed, a damaged man who was more than a bit afraid.

Yet, it wasn't all sunshine and roses. My blog sites had become silent. Attempts to write fell flat, and too often as a result, I retreated into silence. Something was still pushing from the depths, and I was pushing back. It was as if I didn't learn any lessons from the past. I didn't want anything more to mess up what had been rescued and claimed as my life.

On occasion, I had been seen nude by another neighbour, Mary. She had occasionally seen me nude while I was writing at a table on the back deck or working in the back yard while nude. Typically, I would react to her presence with covering up while on the back deck upon realising that she was there, usually after she called out to say hello. It had happened with some regularity.

"This afternoon our neighbour, Mary said "Hi," as she passed by the fence through which I was barely visible while sitting at a table writing while sky clad. Several minutes later, she then came into the yard while I sat, writing. She approached me to ask if she could have some beets from our garden. She made no comment about my nudity. I hadn't expected her to enter the yard after the greeting, so I hadn't covered myself. Getting an affirmative response, she then went into the garden to pick the beets then returned saying thanks as she then left our yard. It seemed as if it was okay to be me, even a nude me."

Our neighbour, Mary had bought all my books, even the three Naked Poetry books, and had read them all. It shouldn't have surprised me that she would accept my nudity without making a fuss. But I did worry that my nudity would somehow negatively affect her friendship with Marynia. However, as was the case with Faye, my nudity didn't create the issue that worried me.

The strangest thing that I am learning as I age, is that time spent clothing free is vital to my well-being. Too many days without conscious time spent nude and my spirit gets very agitated. It's as though I find myself going through a period of withdrawal. Yet as soon as I get to meditate au naturel or be blessed with being bathed with the sun's rays, I find myself in peace and at one with what I can only call "spirit." It almost feels as though I have entered a form of religious ecstasy. Could it be that naturism filled the spiritual vacuum that came with a loss of religious faith?"
[July 11, 2015]

With the Camino only weeks away, and with training having confirmed that they were ready to make the eight-hundred-kilometre pilgrimage, I began to see the Camino not as a physical challenge or as a journey of healing, but more of a spiritual quest. I had to ask, '*Why am I walking?*' It wasn't enough for me to say that it was simply an adventure on our bucket list, the reason we both usually gave to any who asked. The Camino was going to be a testing ground to see if I would find myself worthy. I would find the answers somewhere between Saint Jean Pied de Port and Santiago.

Chapter Thirty – Pilgrims Sharing the Journey

Arriving in Santiago de Compostela, together, October 2015.

We left Canada on August 23, 2015 and arrived in Paris the next morning with the plan of taking an overnight train to Bayonne in the south of France that same night. While in Paris we decided to walk around the Left Bank to pass the long hours between our arrival and the late overnight train. We were both too hyped to sit still very long. Before returning to the train station in the late afternoon, it rained. As a result, we arrived at the train station soaked and tired.

We got to Saint Jean just after the lunch hour, registered for the Camino, and bought scallop shells to put on our backpacks. The scallop was the symbol that would identify us as pilgrims. We were both tired from travelling. However, rather than rest, we decided to go exploring the town. We knew that we wouldn't have been able to sleep anyway. There was too much to see before taking our first steps on the Camino the next morning. Roaming through the picturesque town, we found something to eat, took a lot of photos, and were finally ready to sleep as night fell.

The next morning, on Marynia's sixty-fifth birthday, we began the Camino with a short day of walking to Orisson. Once at our first stop, we made connections with other pilgrims, some of whom would be met again and again until arriving at Santiago de Compostela. With these new friends, we celebrated Marynia's birthday. Thirty-five people sang "Happy Birthday" to her. The Camino had begun well.

The second day, we walked considerably longer than the first day. We arrived in Espinal, Spain, by mid-afternoon. Between the long hike and the heat, we were very tired. On the third day, we walked another twenty-four kilometres with a rest stop in Zubiri en route to Larrasoana. It was our forty-fourth wedding anniversary:

"Here on the Camino we walk within ourselves, our hands holding onto walking poles that click off the kilometres. It's hard work, tiring work. At the end of six or seven hours of walking we are dead tired and want nothing but to shower and perhaps take a rest before we set out to discover the small community which we have chosen for our night's stay. This late afternoon walk around the village was done hand-in-hand, just like the walks we take around our home town. With no poles to occupy our hands, it's as though magnets force our hands to seek each other. The mind doesn't play a role in this – magic is all

that can be said to explain it. I admit it, she still is my Magical Other. " [August 28, 2015]

On the Camino, walking longer distances, we felt very strong, at times walking more than thirty kilometres in a day. As had become a habit, we stopped only when hungry or when our socks needed changing before pushing on. It was as if both of us were obsessed with not wasting time while getting to Santiago. The idea of simply being present had vanished, being replaced with targets of distance and hostels. Of course, when that happens, when one forgets to be present, there is always a price that will be needed to be paid.

When we entered the Meseta, we were surprised to find the first third of the Camino, the period of testing of the body, finished. The second third through the Meseta to Leon, was about testing the mind, the will to complete the work of walking the Camino.

From Leon, with the second third completed, we walked each day, fortified by resolve and by frequent doses of ibuprofen to deaden the aches and pains that became the reality of walking long distances, day-after-day. We reached the Cruz de Fero, the iron cross intending to leave stones carried from Canada. However, seeing tour buses and hordes of pilgrim tourists surrounding the iron cross, we both decided to walk on passed the tall iron cross, to find a quiet rest spot.

> *"A bit further down the trail we found a bench where we could savour the silence and take time to think about our family and why we were walking. We had walked more than 500 kilometres to get this far, suffering and rejoicing at the same time. As we sat there, a small number of pilgrims passed us, all lost in their own thoughts of their own pilgrimages. "* [September 21, 2015]

The cost in terms of pain and the aggravation of injuries made both of us wonder if we would be able to walk the last hundred and seventeen kilometres into Santiago after arriving in Sarria. The next day was the hardest day we had yet endured since beginning the Camino. We were thankful to find a bed in Morgade after walking only seventeen kilometres. It looked and felt as though our Camino was coming to an early end.

The next day, refusing to quit, we began to walk tentatively, ready to have someone call a taxi for the backpacks if the walking got too tough. We walked slowly and gently. The easing of the pace and the lessening of our expectations allowed us to keep going. And with that, our spirits picked up. Paradoxically, the drastic slowing of our walking pace gave us a gift.

"It was another magical day of moon, mist, old oaks, and ancient artifacts of men. As we came down the small mountain, we found ourselves entering the mist. It was a place where there were no shadows, only possibilities. It was a time and place for letting go of certainties, a time and place to accept what is, rather than what the ego says should be." [September 29, 2015]

As we walked the last few days of the Camino, the crowds of pilgrims got larger and noisier. Pilgrims without backpacks passed as if we were standing still. These pilgrims were in a rush to get to the next stop, where often a bus would be waiting for them. I was getting angrier and angrier at these pilgrims who hadn't taken the long route, the path through suffering and pain over hundreds of kilometres, carrying everything needed on their backs. My anger shocked me and Marynia. I suddenly realised that it wasn't the tourist pilgrims who were the problem, I was the one with a problem. I wanted to control their Camino experience rather than focus on my own journey.

The last two days of the Camino were walked in the rain. Soaked to the skin, we laughed as we passed pilgrims huddled under bridges. We walked along the trail which had been turned into a winding creek without complaint. We stopped from time to time to have coffee and meals. Eventually, on the last day, the deluge gave way to a gentle shower as we walked the final kilometres into and through the city of Santiago towards the Cathedral and the pilgrim office in order to get our Camino completion certificates.

It took forty days to walk to Santiago. We both arrived suffering injuries from the long walk. After taking time to dry out and wander around Santiago, we caught a train to the south-east coast of Spain, the Costa del Sol where we would stay at a naturist resort in Estepona. We needed someplace quiet to sit still and rest our bodies. For the next two weeks, there was no need to do any touring, any wandering around towns. We simply sat still, taking advantage of the hot Jacuzzi and a cold swimming pool, followed by soaking up sunshine, or simply relaxing in the quiet condo we had rented.

The two weeks in Estepona gave me time to sort through what had happened on the Camino. Unlike my attempt three years earlier in France, this had become a real Camino for two, as a couple. We had learned to adapt to each other's injuries, pace needs, fatigue, and moods along the way, a mirror of sorts of the life journey we had taken as a couple over forty-four years. The two weeks also gave me time to release tensions that had to do with not having taken any time for meditation or naturism. Being in a naturist site, there was freedom for both.

-

We flew home to Canada at the end of October. And, as other times, we began a whirlwind of travel to catch up with family. I had also begun to write a version of what would be the third book of this autobiography. However, I stopped writing almost as soon as I had begun. I just wasn't ready to write this story. That story had to wait. Instead, I retreated into a writing silence, preferring to invest time in being present in life and with people. And then, emerging out of the cold of winter and seasonal depression, I finally found the voice needed, to begin writing what I believed would be the last part of my story.

I wrote furiously for ten days and then stopped. The need to be present at home was too vital. I needed to be with my family. I also knew that a return to Mexico would allow me the time for the story to be written unimpeded.

Once settled back into the studio at Casa Sorpresas in the New Year, the words began to flow. I finished writing the first draft in mid-February 2016. All during the writing process, I had continued to send Marynia what had been written, hoping that she would spot inconsistencies or missing pieces. I hadn't thought that in reading what I had written, she would respond emotionally. There were tears as old wounds were reopened during the reading. Yet, the words needed to be written and read.

Finally, I believed that the story outlining my life as a husband, father, and grandfather had been finished. At least, that is what I had assumed. It had taken me years of therapy, decades of writing, and a lifetime of hiding to finally realise this truth. Life happened. I had been traumatized. I survived and buried that trauma and lived as though there had never been anything out of the ordinary in my life. I built a new life that didn't have any place in it for the past. I built a life that was centred on others.

I liked feeling undamaged, being competent, being loved and liked in the life I had created. I had even come to believe I was being honest – '*What you see of me is who I am.*' I couldn't change the world, so I had changed myself and lost the truth of who I was in the process. It was as simple as that. The betrayal of myself was the greatest betrayal. Arriving at midlife had changed the rules. It became time to pay the price for putting my soul in solitary confinement. Midlife crisis gave me a choice, to go on a journey of healing, or to call it quits. This book tells the story of that choice and the journey. Like all journeys, I needed guides along the way, and I found them.

How had I managed to get from being wounded as a child, to travel through the breakdown at midlife rendering me incapable of being a husband, father, and teacher, to the place I find myself today? Somehow, though history couldn't be changed, I survived.

So how did all this come about? With mental-health therapy, with taking quiet, introvert time-outs to allow me the energy to be more present with others, with mindful meditation to help quieten a mind that would race away on itself, with naturism and nudity to allow a sense of wholeness and complete control, with stubbornness to resist believing the inner voices that would have me give up, and with a stubborn clinging to love. It wasn't just one path to survival and wellness. It was the full-meal deal, a recipe that was inclusive of all these approaches to healing.

Afterword

I'm in a good place now. I breathe easier and hope that this journey of healing and life will allow me to arrive at the end of the journey with my wits intact. Together with Marynia, the world has taken on different flavours and colours. Both of us have finally accepted that though we are very different, we can thrive by accepting and honouring those differences.

-

The story told here is my story, or should I say, our story. When one is in a relationship, all that is said and done have ripple effects on both oneself and the other person. As I began to fall apart, with little pieces of me falling apart, my wife's world also began to fall apart. And when I dared to begin the long journey of healing, her healing journey began to appear. Because we dared to remain together, we now enter our golden years together.

I had two motives for the telling of this story. The first motive was to ensure that the story was told. It was vital for our children, and in the years to come our grandchildren, to learn that regardless of the trauma that life inflicts upon us, we can make choices to overcome the trauma rather than remain as victims. My second reason was to provide readers with a sense of hope. If I could emerge from the shadows, fear and pain; then perhaps my readers could risk their journey of healing as well.

So, now I am left with outlining the keys that allowed all of this to happen for me.

1. The first key was that I was never really, alone despite what I felt and believed. Very few of us are truly alone, even when we push others away from us.

2. The second key was to reach out for help, mental-health help. It doesn't matter what others think about you. What

matters is that you think about yourself and your survival.

3. The third key for me was to learn about what was happening to me, and never stop learning about depression and the roots of depression.

4. The fourth key was to learn to take time-outs so that I could get relief. For me those time-outs centred around meditation

5. The fifth key for me was tell my story through writing. I told it in my blog posts, my poetry, my novels, and this series of my autobiography. I am still learning that my words touch others

6. The sixth key for me was naturism. Regardless of why I unconsciously slipped into naturism, being nude while I wrote, meditated, read, immersed myself into nature, and spent social time with other naturists – the therapeutic effects were and are real.

7. The seventh key for me is simply, love. I am loved, and I love.

I have tried leaving out one step or the other at times, only to find myself slipping backwards. As a result, I have learned to trust that all these steps are needed if I am to remain mentally healthy and worthy in my own eyes. I have also learned that I had somehow tried to live my life and attempt the journey of healing with others setting the rules and processes, I would have never lived this long. It takes courage to be "self." The will to live, the will to love, the will to be authentically oneself. This is where the journey begins and where it ends.

Acknowledgements

It has taken me years to finally come to realise that my journey of healing needed to embrace all the tools and strategies that were offered to me. I had understood earlier that Buddhist meditation and Jungian psychology had significant roles to play in my healing journey, but the rawness of naturism was something that challenged me and everyone else around me. I have finally learned to honour everything that allows me to be fully present in life.

I don't recommend naturism for others, but I don't rule it out either. Each person is different and must travel their own unique journey of healing, or as Jungians frame it, a journey of individuation. We all have different needs, different wounds, and different broken roads to follow in order to become healthier humans.

No story can come into existence without the direct and indirect influences of others. It is with the guidance of Marvin Haave and Doug Glazer, two Saskatchewan Teachers Federation mental health counsellors that helped me at the beginning of my heroic journey of healing. As well Mae Stolte and Zeljko Matijevic, two Jungian analysts in Calgary, Alberta who gave me their guidance as the journey unfolded. With their collective help, I managed to build a compass which still guides me along this life-long journey of healing.

I must thank most, my wife. Maureen, who gave me the encouragement to write this story. As I gave her bits and pieces to read as the story unfolded, she was honest in her opinions, something any writer needs if a story is to be worth reading. She waited patiently for this work to be done so that the past could finally be laid to rest. And most importantly, I thank her for never giving up on me.

I want to thank my children for never losing faith in me as their father through all the difficult years. They never withdrew from my life, even when I made it difficult. They served as motivation for me to tell this difficult story told in the three books that have made up this series.

I also want to thank the good people of Elrose and Lanigan for supporting both of us as friends and neighbours such as Denise and Wayne Sweet, and Darlene Ellis. We all have a community surrounding us, even when we are not aware of that community. I want to thank Kim Temple, the owner of Casa Sorpresas, for providing me with a sacred sanctuary in Puerto Morelos, Mexico where this book was first written. I want to thank Marcelo Espinoza and Meghan Cox, the owners of Casa Valdivia for renting us their casa for the past two winters where I finally finished the book.

I also have to thank a number of people who read this book as beta readers and proof readers so that the final result which you see here, is less error-filled. Thank you, Robert Payne, Keith Andre, Dustin Longpré, Maureen Longpré and Allen Heggen.

And finally, I want to thank you, the reader, for making it to the end of this journey down a broken road that ended up in a universe filled with light and hope. You as the readers, helped motivate me to write the story. In Jungian psychology, at the end of the journey of individuation, the hero returns bearing gifts for the world he or she had left behind. This is my gift, one of hope for others who are wounded.

Robert G. Longpré, 2019

54005001R00139

Made in the USA
Columbia, SC
24 March 2019